*This book is dedicated to Martha Wright,
whose friendship, wisdom, and persistence
led to the writing of this book.*

# Table of Contents

# Introduction

## PRAYER CHANGES US

Prayer changed me.

That change began on a plane ride to Chicago. I had hopped on the plane to attend a quick conference held over a weekend. To this day, I cannot remember what the conference was about nor what I learned there. What I do recall is my encounter with prayer's ability to change me.

I had not always encountered prayer in this way. In fact, I would say prior to that moment, I was unaware that prayer had any power to change me. Prayer had always felt like a rote discipline, something I knew I was supposed to do but found arduous. On occasion when life was good, I would chat with God, telling God what was going well, thanking God for things, maybe asking for a thing or two. When life took one of its turns for the worse, I would pray asking for things, begging for change, sometimes even demanding it.

That was when I was doing the praying. When others were praying, most of the time I would impatiently wait until the person finished. In church, it felt like the pastor would drone on forever until finally asking us to pray the Lord's Prayer with him. At youth group meetings, I would distract myself from my impatience by counting the number of times the person praying said a name for God. The record holder was a fellow youth group member who managed to say a name for God seventy-two times in about two minutes! I found prayer sometimes not just rote but something to be endured until it was over, when the person praying was finally done talking to God.

For me, that was prayer: talking to God, giving God my needs and occasionally saying thanks, and suffering through other people praying. I felt no special connection to God through prayer. There were times I would hear or read that it was supposed to work that way, but it never did for me. Prayer was just a rote discipline.

8

What good did it do anyway? It didn't seem to change God's mind, especially in the theology that raised me, different from the Methodist theology I believe now. I was raised to think God had already determined everything anyway and my job was to figure out what God had decided for me. So what was the point of asking God to change what God had decided before I was even born? Then I would also hear that prayer changed things. But I never saw prayer change anything, so that was further reason for me to wonder what the point of prayer was.

As I began my career as a pastor, my thoughts on prayer softened. I was no longer impatient, and I no longer thought of it as only rote, but I still I found myself confused about prayer. I had inklings that it was more than rote discipline and even more than talking to God in my head, but had yet to encounter anything different. I wondered, too, what its role was supposed to be in my life and in the life of those I led. It sounds like a funny thing for a pastor to say, but that was where I was on my own faith journey: confused about prayer, knowing it had some power but having not experienced much of it for myself.

That began to change on that plane ride to Chicago.

As we flew, I read a book by Jason Santos titled *A Community Called Taizé*.[1] The chaplain at Mercer University had challenged me to retool the university's chapel service to a contemplative model. I had little experience with contemplative prayer and had never heard of Taizé, but I relished the challenge and wanted to complete the project to satisfy a seminary class requirement. So I picked up the book and found myself enthralled. Here was a community centered around prayer, particularly contemplative prayer, which was new to me. Through Santos's book, I discovered how contemplative prayer had changed the community: They were generous, thoughtful, forgiving, and focused on what really matters in life, in large part because of their regular practice of prayer.

By the time I exited the plane in Chicago, I longed to experience a Taizé service, to experience contemplative prayer within the setting of a worship service. While riding the subway toward conference registration, I searched around for services to attend in Macon when I got back home but could find only one, and it did not work with my schedule.

Upon arriving at Fourth Presbyterian Church in Chicago to check in for the conference, I noticed a flier about a Taizé service happening that evening. I could not believe my luck. After checking in and getting settled in my lodging, I went back to Fourth Presbyterian to attend the service.

There, I experienced the power of prayer as practiced by Taizé, especially the

1. Jason Brian Santos, *A Community Called Taizé: A Story of Prayer, Worship and Reconciliation* (Downers Grove, IL: IVP Books, 2008).

silence that forms the center of the service. I found myself enraptured, pulled in to simply being present, losing sight of all the weights I carried and concerns for tomorrow. In that moment, I experienced joy, peace, and love; my soul found its way home to the heart of Christ. I experienced the power of prayer to change me.

I found, in that Taizé service, what prayer is designed to do: It takes us home to the heart of Christ where our true home lies. On occasion in my life prior to that service, I had experienced such a moment: a powerful worship service, a transfixing sunset, or an enrapturing moment. I recall as a teenager noting my first dance in my Bible, right next to significant spiritual events like confirmation or baptism. Looking back, I marked it because a girl asking me to dance when I thought I was the biggest reject of them all in tenth grade was a tremendous experience of acceptance. But those moments, like that first dance, were fleeting. Discovering contemplative prayer, and discovering the power of prayer to bring me home to the heart of God, showed me how to find my way home on my own, not reliant upon circumstances to do it for me. Prayer changed me.

That first Taizé service was nearly a decade ago. I have remained faithful to contemplative prayer ever since, founding three Taizé services in the meantime and discovering new joys in the daily office and meditation. Prayer continues to change me because it continues to connect me in ever deeper ways with God, revealing how God is calling me, changing my outlook on life, making me more self-aware, and pushing me to greater service for God's kingdom.

For me, contemplative prayer is what works best as a personal prayer practice. By works for me, I mean it provides that sense of connection between me and God, a connection that causes me to experience at times the fruits of the spirit and at other times the sins and rough edges in need of correction and confession. Through experiencing God in this way, I am changed; I grow in Christlikeness as I learn in ever deepening ways what it is to know God's love and experience release from sin and death.

This is what I hope for you from reading this book: that you discover a practice of prayer that changes you. It may be contemplative, it may be another form of prayer, but whatever the form, this book is designed to help you discover how prayer can change you. This will require experimentation, learning new forms of prayer as outlined in the chapters and appendices. Such learning always requires a bit of courage and a spirit of adventure. As you read, I hope you will adopt such a posture, believing all the while that prayer can change you because prayer does, in fact, change us.

We are perhaps accustomed to hearing how prayer changes things or how prayer changes God's mind or how prayer changes life's circumstances. These things are true. There are many books that speak to this part of the power of prayer. I can attest to moments like this from small group settings, Sunday school classes, and worship services. Contrary to my early experience, I have come to learn that prayer does change things, and prayer, it seems, affects the heart of God.

But we must add to this the ways in which we are changed by our regular encounters with God in prayer. How could we not be? To encounter God is to encounter pure holiness, to encounter our creator where we find the deepest resonance of our innermost being, to place our souls humbly before God for refinement. Proverbs says that "as iron sharpens iron, so one person sharpens another" (Prov. 27:17 NIV) The same is true for our relationship with God: We are shaped and molded by our encounters with God. Sometimes, it comes with the friction and sparks of iron sharpening iron, sometimes it comes through an encounter with holy comfort, but regardless, we are changed.

And we are changed not for self-improvement, not for an easier life, but for the mission of the kingdom of God. Prayer changes us by refining our rough edges, convicting us of sin, calling us to God's will, bringing us ever deeper into the heart of Christ where God's unconditional love lives. This book is not a self-help scheme, providing a prayerful means to make life better. A less stressful, more joyous life may indeed be a result, but it is not the point. The point, as we Methodists describe it, is to walk farther down the path of sanctification, growing in holiness. We will discuss more about that in chapter 1. When we allow ourselves to be changed by prayer, engaging in regular prayer practice, we become powerful missioners for the kingdom of God, revealing Christ into the world as we grow closer to his heart.

The author Henri Nouwen puts it well, as quoted in the daily office prayer book *Common Prayer*, "'Praying is no easy matter. It demands a relationship in which you allow someone other than yourself to enter into the very center of your person, to see there what you would rather leave in darkness, and to touch there what you would rather leave untouched.'"[2] To engage in prayer that changes us requires our willingness to be changed by our encounters with God, sometimes meaning that we will go through experiences of suffering. But we have the comfort and promise that God is working in our lives, redeeming our suffering, bringing us into the light. Once we have emerged on the other side, we will reveal even more of Christ to the world because we will be better acquainted with his heart.

In my time as a pastor, I have encountered many who long to pray well and often but struggle to figure out how to do so. If that sounds like your journey, this book is for you. I have found others who say they pray on a regular basis but that their prayers just feel empty or that they "don't work." If that sounds like your journey, this book is also for you. I have been there in my own journey, struggling to pray,

2. Henri Nouwen, in an uncited quotation in Shane Claiborne, Jonathan Wilson-Hartgrove, and Enuma Okoro, *Common Prayer: A Liturgy for Ordinary Radicals* (Grand Rapids, MI: Zondervan, 2010), 449.

forcing myself to pray on a regular basis, all the while wondering why it felt so empty and purposeless. Wasn't I supposed to feel something as a result? Know God better somehow?

The answer is yes, we are. When our focus while learning to pray is on how prayer changes things or on how prayer can change the heart of God, we are entering into the learning process with the wrong mindset. Prayer is first and foremost an act of our hearts, calling out to God's heart. The psalmist says, "deep calls to deep." (Ps. 42:7) That is a great definition of prayer, the depths of our souls calling out to God. So while prayer does change things and while prayer can have an impact on God's work in the world, we as disciples of Christ should begin with the experiential side of prayer, discovering how prayer connects us to God in deep and profound ways that change us.

Even after that Taizé service at Fourth Presbyterian, I have continued to have questions about prayer. That day was a milestone on my journey of faith, and I have continued down that path, exploring the power of prayer ever since. What I have discovered so far on that journey is catalogued in this book. It is by no means exhaustive, and in some ways it barely scratches the surface, but it is a sharing of my journey with you, the reader, in the hopes that the sharing of my journey can help you on your own journey. When you ask those same questions about prayer, wondering what its point is, wondering how it's supposed to help you feel something or know God better, my hope and prayer is this book helps you find the answers, or at least the beginning of the answer.

Finding the answer starts with understanding what prayer is and the forms it takes. There are many ways to pray, illuminated in chapters to come. Much of the content centers around helping us give attention to prayer. How often have you found your mind wandering when someone else is praying? Holding our attention is very difficult! It requires giving our full attention to the prayer itself and to the Holy Spirit speaking inside of us. Educator and philosopher Simone Weil says, "Prayer consists of attention. It is the orientation of all the attention of which the soul is capable toward God. The quality of the attention counts for much in the quality of prayer."[3] I hope that through this reading, you will discover practical tips to holding and giving your attention by finding a pathway of prayer that works for you. Once so discovered, I hope you will find that sense of connection to God whereby we are changed.

This book is designed to be a resource book; a practical guide to discovering the power of prayer to change us through finding a pathway of prayer that works for you. To that end, this book opens with a chapter on the grounding of prayer:

---

3. Simone Weil, *Waiting for God*, trans. Emma Craufurd (New York: Harper Perennial, 1951), 57.

relationship with Christ and the pursuit of holiness. Chapters 2 through 7 continue to teach how we are to pray by offering practical tips, such as finding routine, using repetition, and praying with authenticity. The next set of chapters, 8 through 13, teach how prayer changes us, such as in teaching a faith that can say "even if," deepening our self-awareness, and helping us learn to hear the voice of God over the din of all the other voices and noises we encounter. The conclusion then gives direction for creating your own practice of prayer.

Each chapter includes a suggested scripture reading, the inspiration for the chapter itself. I recommend reading the scripture and allowing it to be open nearby for reference as you read the chapter. Our reading of scripture should inform all that we do when we engage with God, including our prayer lives. This book operates no differently.

In some chapters, I refer to specific practices of prayer or other resources that you may find helpful in the journey. These are included in the appendix. Some of those resources I developed for congregations I have served, others were developed specifically for this book, but in all cases they are designed to be used. In the end, I hope the use of those materials leaves this book looking worn because it has proved to be a reference guide and encouragement for establishing a routine of daily prayer that changes you.

Such a routine brings us to our true homes: the heart of Christ. A well-worn, oft-trod pathway of prayer helps us get there when life is difficult and challenges arise. Thus, it's critical that we form a habit of prayer while times are good and things seem easy, which is, of course, the times when we're least likely to pray.

So with all this in mind, let us begin. We embark on a journey here in the text, a journey of exploration and learning. I pray with you and for you that the journey leads you closer to the heart of Christ, where our true homes are, as we are changed for the better by our experience of prayer.

To begin this conversation on prayer changing us, we start with the basics of the Christian life: the call to holiness and the role of prayer in shaping that holiness. The journey of faith is the grounding of prayer; one formed in our relationship with Christ.

With all this in mind, let us begin.

# Part 1: How to Pray

# Chapter 1

## RELATIONSHIP OVER RULES

*Scripture Reading: Leviticus 19:1-2, 19:9-18*

Francis Flournoy was a Kentucky farmer with an opinion. Day after day, he tended to the crops on his fields in the hills of Kentucky. Night after night, he thought about his new country. Day after day, he worked tirelessly. Night after night, he pondered fearlessly.

On his Kentucky farm, among the rolling hills, Flournoy could look out and see the entire world. While sitting on the front porch, he could see the geopolitical dynamics of the world's powers at play. On the back of his horse, he could see the intricate interplay of the world's economic systems. Flournoy "lived and moved and had [his] being" (Acts 17:28) at a crucial time in American history, at the turn of the nineteenth century.

If there's one thing Flournoy understood, it was land. He had tilled the land his whole life; he had given his blood, sweat, and tears to it; and so he properly understood its value. And he knew the land next door to Kentucky needed to be allied with France.

So he wrote an op-ed to the Frankfort Guardian of Freedom, a local newspaper.[1] Well, an op-ed is being kind. It was an open letter to the French government, particularly its emperor, Napoleon Bonaparte, on behalf of this private American citizen. This open letter asked the French to establish a new colony west of Kentucky. In 1803, when Flournoy wrote his open letter, this French-owned land was known as the Louisiana Territory.

---

1. Wilson C. Freeman, "The Logan Act: An Overview of a Sometimes Forgotten 18th Century Law," *Congressional Research Service*, https://fas.org/sgp/crs/misc/LSB10058.pdf, accessed August 11, 2020.

Flournoy's letter attracted some attention, particularly the attention of James Blair, Kentucky's attorney general, who indicted Flournoy for violating the Logan Act. Enacted in 1799 by the fifth Congress and signed by President John Adams, the Logan Act forbids private citizens from engaging in diplomacy with foreign governments. Flournoy found himself charged with committing a felony for his open letter to the French government in the Frankfort Guardian of Freedom.

Later in that same year of 1803, President Thomas Jefferson purchased the Louisiana Territory in an act called the Louisiana Purchase. This purchase removed France's territorial claims on this content, making the indictment against Flournoy moot in the eyes of Attorney General Blair, so charges were dropped.

But not before Francis Flournoy, a simple American farmer with an opinion and mind for geopolitics went down in history as the only person ever to be indicted for violating the 1799 Logan Act.

Stories about the impacts of the law are interesting, sometimes even fascinating. Who doesn't love a "who done it?" story or a legal thriller. But laws themselves are rather boring. Who would get a copy of the United States Code to read for fun? Much less, who would read Leviticus for fun, a book of the law sometimes compared to the US Code?

While it sounds dry and boring, like most laws, inside Leviticus is a captivating story of love and the interplay between God and humanity such as is found in this chapter's Scripture reading from Leviticus 19.

The law in that scripture, and in much of Leviticus, is about governing behavior and setting standards and expectations. Where someone violates the law, like Francis Flournoy, there are consequences to those actions. And so the law is, generally, a tool of negative reinforcement: We're afraid of the consequences of breaking the law, so we choose to follow it out of respect and fear.

That's the traditional view of biblical law: fear that God would come down with curses and dire consequences for failure to uphold it. It's true for us with respect to the laws of our country, for we don't want to go to jail or pay fines. And sometimes, it's true for us as Christians, fearing what will happen if we fail to live a good, moral, life—in other words, if we fail to obey the teachings of Jesus and the Bible.

I was reminded of that fear when I saw a billboard recently. Perhaps you've seen it on the interstate, too. It says, very simply, "Real Christians Obey Jesus's Teachings," followed by a toll-free number.

When I saw it, I wondered, which teachings did they mean? Some of Jesus's teachings seem easy, like love each other, be a peacemaker. Others are more difficult, like don't get divorced, sell everything you own and give it to the poor, or open your home to strangers. Surely, these folks don't mean all of Jesus's teachings?

Some Christians talk of Jesus's teachings like laws. If we break Jesus's laws, we face consequences of separation in our relationship with God. For these Christians, failure to uphold the law of Jesus causes us to experience less of who God is and know God's love in a diminished capacity.

For them, Jesus's teachings are a form of negative reinforcement. They are behavioral standards by which we are to abide, lest we face the consequences. Like Francis Flournoy and the Logan Act, we must uphold Jesus's law out of fear of the consequences of breaking it.

Maybe we disagree, but let's consider how we live our lives for a second. Very often, we're concerned about doing the wrong thing. We're worried about our behavior and wondering if it jives with what the Bible teaches. Growing up in church taught us that we're supposed to be good people, lead moral lives, set the example, do the right thing. And when we fail to live up to that standard, church might have also taught us that we run the risk of, at best, God's disappointment with us and guilt in that relationship or, at worst, God's vengeance set against us.

And so it's tempting and perhaps normal to focus heavily on what it means to practice morality, to be good, to do the right thing, because we fear falling out of God's good graces. The teachings of Jesus, then, become a law no different than the Logan Act or the rest of the US Code.

That's how I grew up. Maybe you can relate. Maybe you think of Christianity in the same way: It's a set of rules. Go to church, don't lie, don't steal, tithe.

If that doesn't sound like Christianity, or if it does sound like Christianity but you don't like it, what's the alternative? What does it mean to be a Christian if it's not about following the rules to stay in good relationship with God—in other words, to be holy? That's the pursuit, after all. We want the same thing that Leviticus declares: to be holy. The law in Leviticus is about being holy as God is holy, just as Jesus's teachings are about being holy just as God is holy. Doesn't that mean following a set of standards, a set of rules?

The answer to that question is why I love Leviticus.

Leviticus is a love letter from God.

That may sound odd, for whom would rightly call a set of laws a love letter? But, indeed, Leviticus forms a love letter from God to us.

Leviticus contains more words directly from the mouth of God than any other book in the Bible. Throughout this book, codified as law, God reveals who God is and what God cares about. In other words, God directly shares more of God's heart in Leviticus than perhaps anywhere else in scripture; it's a love letter from God. We can relate this to parents giving rules to children to provide structure and boundaries, revealing what is valued: things essential for children to thrive. Parents who do this well also reveal and instill good, healthy values in their children. Here in Leviticus, we find our divine parent defining boundaries and setting rules, creating the conditions for God's children to thrive just like a good parent.

So let's take a deeper look at the scripture referenced at the start of this chapter to see how God is revealing that heart to us.

Throughout the ten verses referenced at the start of the chapter, God reveals that God cares deeply about the poor, the laborer, the deaf, the blind, and the immigrant (known as the "alien" often in translations of Leviticus). God speaks of the need for fairness before the law, of justice for all, and of loving each other as neighbors and family.

In God's heart, the poor are of paramount concern. Rather than allowing them to go hungry, God commands that the people leave the edges of their fields for the poor to come and get the food they need, free of charge. This is called gleaning, and it's the inspiration for a practice at a church I served. There, on the fourth Sunday, children pass around baskets and church members give of whatever cash they happen to have on them. The proceeds support the local backpack buddy program addressing childhood hunger.

In God's heart, immigrants are of paramount concern. In ancient Israelite society, as in societies for ages, foreigners were regarded with suspicion. They were suspect, they were strange, their culture seemed threatening to the dominant culture, and so people would shun them, ignore them, and even commit violent acts against these immigrants. God says no, they're your neighbors, too. Take care of the immigrants among you as if they were your family.

In God's heart, the deaf and the blind are of paramount concern. Ancient societies tended to shun them, even kill them or run them out of cities to live on their own because those with disfigurations and those with developmental disabilities were regarded as punished by God, so many worried that their presence would elicit God's anger. No, God says, I love them, too, and they're your neighbors.

In God's heart, the laborer is of paramount concern. Don't delay in making payments for work done, God says, and be generous about it, for the laborer is your neighbor, even to be regarded as your kin.

These examples from Leviticus are found elsewhere throughout scripture. And they are reinforced by Jesus throughout the Gospels and especially in the Sermon on the Mount. They reveal to us that God's heart is all about love: love for all people at all times and in all places. God's heart is also about justice: fairness in treatment for all people, especially those oppressed by society, even the ones we tend to shun and even the ones we find scary. God's heart is about peace, all people living in harmony together, no matter their differences, no matter what, for we are all neighbors and all God's kin.

This is the message of Leviticus. It's a message that resonates across scripture and can be summed up by Jesus's declaration of the first and second greatest commandments: love God, and love your neighbor as yourself, just as it says here in Leviticus (Lev. 19:17-18).

Holiness is about living in such a loving relationship with God that, through us, God is able to make the world holy: a place of justice for the poor and immigrant and laborer, a place of peace between all neighbors, a place of honest love among all people, no matter their differences.

The pursuit of holiness is the pursuit of a just, peaceful, world—the world God is striving to create through us, a world we call the kingdom of God.

When we choose to try to follow Jesus's teachings, like the billboard describes, expecting that to make us more holy and more in love with God, we put the cart ahead of the horse. We must first get to know God by getting to know God's heart. Then, we will more naturally live out the law, fulfilling God's expectations on our lives. The beginning of obeying Jesus's teaching, the beginning of living according to God's standards, the beginning of holiness, is in prayer. Through these we get to know God better.

Holiness begins not with ritual or rote obedience but, instead, in prayer, for prayer changes us by making us more holy.

If you've been living a life of following rules, wanting to be in relationship with God in that way, stop. God says to us today, "Simply say to me 'I want to know you more,' and you'll discover who I am." Commit yourself to prayer instead, specifically those words of telling God you want to know God better.

Or if you've been reading the Bible as a set of rules, looking for regulations about how to live your life, stop. Pick it up again, but this time, read it as a love letter from God. Ask yourself as you read, "What's God telling me about himself here?" I think you'll discover scripture opens up to you afresh and anew. Then pray back to God what you've discovered. This particular form of prayer is called Lectio Divina (Latin for divine reading) and is an ancient way of praying scripture. (See Appendix 1 for details and Appendix 5 for a schedule of daily scripture readings to use with Lectio Divina.)

God ultimately desires relationship with us. That comes less through rule following and much more through getting to know the heart of God. And the best way to do that is prayer. In this way, prayer changes us. Through a commitment to pray, we get to know God more and more and thus become more and more holy, a reflection of God on earth. Holiness begins not in following rules and regulations but in relationship with God. And that relationship finds grounding in conversation—what we call prayer.

Holiness is what we're after: purity of heart such that, through us, God creates a just world.

Holiness comes not through keeping up with a set of rules but through being in love with God through prayer. It's that simple.

How well does that describe your life? For that's the message of Leviticus. As the three general rules of The United Methodist Church state: do no harm, do good, stay in love with God. That's the love letter from God's heart to us. That's the freedom of relationship with God. Reach out and tell God you want to know him better. Commit to prayer and find the relationship with God you've been seeking.

# Chapter 2

## THE POWER OF ROUTINE IN PRAYER

*Scripture Reading: Psalm 40*

Prayer begins with holiness; with being in love with God. This requires relationship, not simply following a bunch of rules. Once we have established such a relationship, we must learn to be disciplined in that practice of prayer. But why establish a routine? That's where we turn in this next chapter on how to pray. Let us begin.

For many years, a famous band, U2, ended its concerts with a song based on Psalm 40, the very same psalm as the focus text for this chapter. It is one of their most well-known songs, yet it almost didn't happen. As they wrapped up their recording session, they needed to quickly record one more song before releasing their latest album. The lead singer, looking for inspiration, grabbed a Bible nearby and found Psalm 40. Thus was born one of their most enduring hits.

The song opens up with the words of the psalm itself, "I waited patiently for the Lord; he inclined and heard my cry. He lifted me up out of the pit, out of the miry clay. And I will sing, sing a new song." But then it shifts to ask the classic rhetorical question offered throughout many of the psalms: "How long?"

It's a catchy tune, but the song sounds paradoxical. "I waited patiently ... how long? [God] lifted me up out of the pit ... but how long?" I spent many years confused by this song. In its paradoxical nature, waiting patiently while asking how long, it seems to say: I believe; help my unbelief.

So says the father of a boy racked by an evil spirit. He approaches Jesus, looking for help, and says to him, "If you are able" (Mark 9:22b). Jesus responds with shock: "If I am able!–All things can be done for the one who believes" (Mark 9:23). The father then responds with a famous line, echoed for centuries by early Christian bishops and theologians: "I believe; help my unbelief."

It sounds paradoxical. But there it is, Mark 9:24: "I believe; help my unbelief." This is not unlike the sentiment of the author of Psalm 40 who also says in his eloquent language: I believe; help my unbelief.

It was also a common refrain in the first few centuries of Christianity. In the deserts of Egypt in the years after Jesus's resurrection, a community of monks formed. It was in studying them that I first came to hear this ancient statement from Mark 9:24. The Ancient Desert Fathers, as they're known, uttered the verse as a prayer: I believe; help my unbelief. These fathers were mostly very weird. They stood on top of pillars for months on end, they hid themselves in caves and refused to come out, they ate bugs or went on forty-day fasts consuming nothing but water. And all in the desert heat!

They would do things that pushed the boundaries of human limits, seeking a deeper faith. They would purposefully test themselves in crazy ways, things that I would never recommend, in order to stretch their faith. They purposefully caused their own suffering in order to prove that they had faith. And in the midst of such proving they would pray: I believe; help my unbelief.

I recall sitting in the classroom, laughing to myself about this phrase, for it sounded like what I might have said just about anytime I took on a home improvement project. I did not grow up in a household that owned a home. My dad was in charge of all the residence halls at Berry College, so we lived in an apartment in a dorm. I lived in a residence hall until I was 25 and moved into my first house, ever, when I was 26, never learning basic home improvement skills. But being the scrappy, cheapskate guy I can be, I decided I would do whatever repairs or improvements needed to be done by myself.

Often, this decision led me to hours of frustration and failure. Perhaps the most infamous, at least in my wife, Dana's, mind, is the day I decided to install a ceiling fan in our kitchen. That required opening up the ceiling in the middle of the kitchen and running new electrical wire. So I turned off the power to the kitchen and rerouted the wires from a superfluous ceiling light about six feet over to where I wanted the fan. But I ran into a problem. How would I cut open the ceiling? I didn't own a saw.

But I figured one blade was as good as any, so I took a steak knife and jabbed it into the drywall ceiling. I quickly found a joist and cut a square around it. I then set to work on the electrical, which proved more difficult than expected. The sun started to go down as I worked. It got darker and darker in the room. Then, hanging the motor proved more difficult than I expected. Finally, as darkness settled in and the power to the kitchen was still off, Dana, very pregnant with our oldest son, Jackson, told me she'd had enough and I was taking her to get Mexican food that very minute.

But by that time, I wasn't sure if I could handle this project anyway. I wasn't sure I had the right electrical knowledge, the basic knowledge of how to attach a fan to a joist, nor even the basic tools, like a saw, to accomplish the job. I had lost confidence, belief, that I was capable.

This pattern emerged over and over again whenever I would take on a house project. I believed I could do it. And then, as the project got more complicated and more problems emerged, I would stop believing I could do it. Not unlike that ancient prayer, "I believe; help my unbelief."

Such is the case for the author of Psalm 40. Within the first ten verses, he clearly believes. He's seen God's restoration, he knows of reorientation firsthand. God has inclined, drawn him up, set his feet upon a rock, secured his steps, put a new song in his mouth. Because of this, he says happy are those who trust God, who understand that God will provide, will reorient.

In fact, he even thanks God for this restoration, for it has deepened his faith and his understanding of who God is. He tells us this in verses 6 through 8, when declares what the prophet Micah knew well: God does not desire merely right sacrifice but rather a right heart: "to do justice, and to love kindness, and to walk humbly with your God" (Mic. 6:8). A life lived rightly with God, including giving thanks for bringing us through the darkness, should lead to more justice, more love and kindness, and more humility.

The psalmist knows this more acutely than he did before reorientation. His faith has developed, strengthened, deepened, by his prior disorientation. But then, in a surprising turn, the psalmist declares, in verse 11, that he's in trouble. Evils have encompassed, iniquities threaten to overtake him, and he needs deliverance, salvation from his enemies. He asks God to humiliate his enemies.

But he's not convinced that God will come. "Do not, O Lord, withhold your mercy from me … . Be pleased, O Lord, to deliver me … . You are my help and deliverer; do not delay, O my God" (Ps. 40:11, 40:13, 40:17b NRSV). No matter the belief inspired by his previous darkness, this new disorientation leaves him with some doubt. Will God save? Will God provide? Will God deliver?

It's fair to say that, in the first ten verses, the psalmist believes. And then, in verses 11 through 17, he says, "Help my unbelief."

I believe; help my unbelief.

This comes as a part of a cycle of faith where we find ourselves stable, then suddenly unstable, and then surprisingly stable again, although in a new way. God's restoration never recovers the past, for the past can never be again. Instead, reorientation, that new way, brings forth a surprising new work that is better than the past, better than what we could have asked for or imagined. God's work redeems the time of instability.

In teaching that cycle, it's the darkness, the time of instability, that resonates with most folks. The darkness is such a common phenomenon for so many of us. It comes on suddenly, and much more often than we'd like. It's hard to believe in the dark times, which is why we've talked about discipline being more important in times of orientation than disorientation. Such regular practice reinforces beliefs and helps us find the light of God when the darkness settles in.

And yet, sometimes no matter how disciplined we are, the darkness rattles our beliefs, bringing forth doubt. What do we do when our belief is shaken? Or worse, what do we do when our belief is under assault? In the latter half of this psalm, the author is struggling with that very question. He knows that God has provided in the past, he knows of God's restoration and reorientation, but will it happen again? Will God come through again? He's trying to rest securely in the knowledge of what God has done in the past, but his present disorientation means he's not completely convinced, has some doubt, about whether God will redeem, restore, and set free again—whether reorientation will come.

He has doubt. We can hear him saying in that ancient prayer, "I believe; help my unbelief!"

And isn't this our story, too? Especially in the dark times of life, the doubt can seem to take over.

When we describe our life with God as having valleys and mountaintops and plateaus, what we're really describing is our belief. It waxes and wanes with our life's experience. When times are good, it's easy to believe. When God has just delivered us and restored us, it's even easier to believe. But when times are hard, when the darkness settles in, it becomes challenging to believe.

And God redeems such times. That's how we're formed, how our belief is deepened, how we come to understand God better and grow in Christlikeness: When we go through the valleys of doubt, when belief is challenged and we experience doubt, God uses those times to deepen our belief. That's part of the promise of redemption.

But notice I've said belief, not faith. Belief is an act of the mind: willingly choosing to place trust that something is true and right. That trust can easily come under assault and, when it does, the result is doubt. But faith is a posture, not simply an act of the mind. Faith is more than belief: It's belief and practice.

And when belief wanes, when disbelief or doubt settles in, practice can remain.

That's what I understand that rock band to mean by its song based on Psalm 40. That's what this psalm means. And that's what the father with the sick boy meant when he first uttered these words to Jesus: "I believe; help my unbelief." Such a statement is powerful, for it confesses that there's doubt, but that the person will continue to practice, continue in prayer, like he believes anyway.

When we say: "I believe; help my unbelief," we mean, "I'm not sure what's true anymore, but I'm going to keep practicing, praying, like it is true."

In all matters of home repair, I learned by experience. I often had doubt about whether or not I could finish a project, or really accomplish what I set out to accomplish. But no matter the doubt I had, I kept practicing, kept trying, kept working at it.

And in the hard times of life, my spiritual disciplines have worked the same way. I keep practicing, even when there's doubt. Sometimes I wonder why I'm sitting down to pray again when I'm getting no response and the channel between God and me feels dead. Sometimes I wonder how long I'll have to sing my song of despair and fear. Sometimes I wonder if my labor as a pastor is really worth it. Sometimes I have doubt. But I keep practicing.

In modern parlance, we might be tempted to say this is the "fake it until you make it" idea, except we're not faking it. Our hearts still believe, even if our minds are full of doubt. Practice keeps our hearts in line with God until our minds are reoriented to belief. Prayer keeps us at home with Christ.

It's like when I was learning to play the trombone. For months, I simply wasn't getting it. Teachers and other students pointed out that I had my mouth in the wrong place on the mouthpiece, that I was curling the edges of my lips up instead of down, that I was doing my breathing wrong. I tried to fix all of that, but I kept failing; I just wasn't getting it.

Until one day, suddenly, I got it. I could play. My mouth conformed to what it needed to do and I moved forward in my ability to play music. From that moment on, I enjoyed playing and knew that I could do it. But for quite a while there, I wondered if I'd ever be able to play, if I'd ever understand, or if I should just give up.

That's the temptation during the dark times: to give up. When belief fails, when doubt settles in, it's tempting to give up practice, too, to halt our prayer life. What good are they doing, anyway?

Turns out, our discipline in prayer is doing quite a lot of good. When times get tough, when the darkness settles in and doubt crowds out our beliefs, if we will keep practicing, keep praying, we will find they reap a harvest of belief down the road. Practice often precedes belief. And, indeed, practice can lead to belief. But above all, practice, spiritual discipline, keeps our hearts at home with Christ until our minds are reoriented to belief.

There's a cycle to the life of faith. Biblical scholar Walter Brueggemann describes this cycle as orientation, disorientation, and reorientation.[1] During times of orientation, life is stable and we feel little challenge to our faith. Disorientation comes

---

. Walter Brueggemann, *The Message of the Psalms: A Theological Commentary* (Minneapolis, MN: Augsburg Fortress Press, 1984), 19.

along, usually suddenly, when something in life challenges our notions of faith, rocking our stability and giving rise to doubt. These are dark times, the hard moments of life, where our faith is grown when we continue to attend to our practice of prayer. Then one day, the challenges are over and we emerge back into a place of stability in our faith. This is called reorientation, but it is not simply a return to the old orientation. No, it is new because the stability we know after a period of disorientation is marked by a faith deepened by having gone through the dark valley and emerged on the other side.

The trick to the life of faith, whether we're in orientation, disorientation, or reorientation, is to keep practicing. Our belief may have mountaintops and valleys, but our practices can keep us grounded, stable, at home in the heart of Christ, no matter the highs and lows of our belief.

That is the example of the Psalms, all 150 of them. They are full of exuberance, joy, thanksgiving, and hope, just as they are also full of doubt, questions, despair, and anger. But no matter the emotion, no matter the content, even the violent urges that live within a few psalms and even when doubt is present, all of it is offered as a prayer to God. That's the magic of the Psalms. In providing us with examples of how to pray across a broad spectrum of emotion and human existence, the Psalms form a prayer guide for our lives. This is why this book recommends praying the Psalms daily. (See Appendix 4 for a schedule to pray the Psalms daily.)

The message the Psalms give us for living life with God is this: No matter what we're feeling, no matter how wonderful or how terrible, take it in prayer to God.

Even if you're not sure that God is listening, take it in prayer to God.

Even if you're angry with God, take it in prayer to God.

Even if you aren't sure God exists, take it in prayer to God.

No matter the excuses, take it in prayer to God.

Pray, seek after God with your whole heart, in the highs and lows of life, no matter what.

Practice, a regular prayer life, is essential to life with God. During times of orientation, it prepares us for the darkness of disorientation. During disorientation, it keeps us grounded in God and prepares us to see what God is doing as God redeems our experiences. When we know redemption, it gives us the means to return thanks to God for the marvelous deliverance we've experienced. That's stability in life, a stability gained through a regular prayer life.

So wherever you find yourself on the journey of faith, in stability, darkness, or knowing God's redemption, make your prayer this: "I believe; help my unbelief." Such a statement is powerful, for it confesses that even though there's doubt, we will act like we believe anyway. It's a firm commitment of the heart that, even if our head may waver, our heart remains firmly at home with Christ. Make sure you've got a prayer practice that's consistent, a vital part of your life. That's how prayer changes us: it helps us find our footing no matter if life is full of light, darkness, or a mixture of the two.

For it is practice that creates belief, no matter the difficulties we experience in this life. It's practicing prayer that will keep our hearts tuned to God, such that we will never be moved. No matter where you are in life, pray with those who have come before you:

I believe; help my unbelief.

# Chapter 3

## FINDING OUR WAY IN THE DARKNESS

### Scripture Reading: Psalm 15

Prayer keeps us stable when life would throw us off course. The regular discipline and routine of prayer attunes us to the heart of God as we walk the pathway of prayer back to our true homes over and over again. But what do ve do when the light dims and it's hard to find the pathway again? That's where we'll urn next in this chapter.

Let us begin.

I went to the doctor not long after a recent Christmas for a checkup. As we were alking, he patted me on the belly and said, "How's your diet lately?"

I laughed and said, "The holidays were good to me."

He was not amused as he asked me, "Are you sure about that?"

I knew I'd put on some weight over the holidays. I thoroughly enjoyed myself! Times were good with the parties we attended, the people we visited, the food we te, the times of relaxation and rest. I was less active, ate more, drank more, and thus horoughly enjoyed myself.

The end result: weight gain. My disciplines around diet and exercise slipped, and ept slipping, as I was busy with parties and people visiting. Such is the case with the holidays. So I told my doctor, "I have a plan."

My health, besides needing to lose some weight, is excellent. But he reminded ne that weight complicates health and, should I not lose weight, and especially if I gained some more, it could complicate my health and my body would find it harder o fend off disease. So, while times are good and I'm healthy, it's time to lose weight. And that's what I'm doing for my long-term health.

When times are good, it's easy to let disciplines slip. Many of us, myself included when it comes to diet and exercise, need something to motivate us to maintain our disciplines. My guess is, when we think of our prayer, the same is even more true. When life is good, it's easy to let our disciplines of faith slip or simply be nonexistent. But then, when the storms come and we are shaken, we rush back to the disciplines, expecting them to help.

All too often, those disciplines fail to provide as much help as expected. It's no different than experiencing illness caused or complicated by weight and then deciding, while sick, that it's time to lose weight. By then, it can't do as much good as if we'd been disciplined while healthy.

Discipline in prayer is like how we handle our health. Consider that, right after Sept. 11, 2001, churches filled to the brim. In the midst of unimaginable tragedy, people packed church pews. I remember hearing commentators and clergypersons alike stating that this was the renewal moment for the church; this was when we'd reverse the decline in worship attendance and church membership.

But, after about three weeks, the gains evaporated. Many said modern churches were to blame: They were ill-equipped to convince people to stay, they were not seeker-sensitive, they were full of cliques and thus not welcoming. There were all the reasons to think that the church was to blame. And some of that feedback makes sense.

The people themselves, however, offer some explanation, too. They came to church, either found answers they sought, comfort they needed, or not, and then left. Regardless, life went back to usual, stability returned to their lives, and they no longer felt the need for church. They used church to feel better, the way we use aspirin to dull pain.

If we're honest, this is true for some of us, too. When life is good, we don't go to church as often because we just don't think we need it. Things are great, so it's less necessary. Or even if we're convinced it's still necessary, the motivation isn't there like it is when things are hard. And so discipline slips; we don't come to church as much. We treat prayer the same way, calling upon God in the hard times and neglecting our divine-human conversation during the good.

That is, until we're shaken by the next tragedy, the next downturn, the next stressor. When it comes, we rush back to church thinking that church has magic powers to return us to stability. Sometimes, we find comfort in our habit, but most of the time, church and prayer fail to magically restore us to stability in life.

We tend to use church and prayer like we use aspirin: I have a pain in my life, so I take some medicine. But when I don't have the pain, I don't need it, so it sits on the shelf in the cabinet unused. But church isn't like that. Our faith isn't like that. Prayer isn't like that.

We all want the promise of the end of Psalm 15, "Those who do these things shall never be moved." The word "moved" there can be translated as "shaken" or "terror-ized," with the verse thus reading, "those who do these things shall never be shaken" or "never be terrorized." That sounds like a great life, so what are the things we need to do? Clearly, church and prayer as aspirin doesn't work, so how do we realize the promise of Psalm 15 for ourselves?

The psalm reads like a checklist of things to be disciplined about so we won't be moved or terrorized. In fact, there are eleven items we are to check off. It seems that if we accomplish these things on a regular basis, if we're faithful in these eleven things, we will "never be moved/shaken/terrorized."

First, walk blamelessly.
Second, do what's right.
Third, speak the truth from your heart.
Fourth, don't slander with your tongue.
Fifth, do no evil to your friends.
Sixth, don't rebuke your neighbors.
Seventh, despise the wicked.
Eighth, honor those who respect God.
Ninth, stand by your oath even if it hurts you.
Tenth, with apologies to the bankers reading along, don't lend money at interest.
Eleventh, don't accept a bribe if the person is innocent.

Stay true to all those things and you will "never be moved/shaken/terrorized." And, according to verse 1, if you're perfect at all these things, you will be welcomed into worship and into church. Otherwise, you're not welcomed because you're not disciplined enough.

For all those achievement-oriented, type-A folks, here's your checklist for living life with God. If you accomplish these things, you'll be in great shape, for you'll "never be moved/shaken/terrorized."

Except, who can keep all this? If these are the conditions for gaining entry to worship and church, none of us should be there. In a given week, I probably spoke impatiently to others. I didn't lend money at interest, but I probably paid money against an interest-bearing loan, which means that I didn't do what's right. I'm pretty sure, however, that I've never taken a bribe against an innocent person, so I'm clear on one of the eleven! But in sum, I have failed to keep the eleven standards.

This cannot be a checklist. If it was, we would all be in violation. Plus, we have already seen that God wants relationship over rote obedience. Even still, there's truth here for us. So what is that truth? How do we gain access to God's presence, what the author means by verse 1, "Who may abide in your tent? Who may dwell on your holy hill?" How do we live a life where we are never moved/shaken/terrorized?

At twenty-one years old, I was at my heaviest. I also had a brand-new iPod, back when iPods were the hip new thing. It was loaded up with all the music I had and a fancy pair of those earbuds. I was ready to do something with the iPod, but what? I was also really starting to feel guilty about being twenty-one and out of shape. I would get winded going up two flights of stairs to attend class. That just seemed ridiculous.

I was also experiencing emotional stress. Life had challenged long-held assumptions and I felt an instability in my sense of self. That instability created stress and that stress yelled, "Move!" So that's what I did.

Long before Couch to 5K was a thing, I made up my own. I grabbed my iPod, put in the earbuds, and started running one night. I got about ten yards and was out of breath. But I kept moving. I had picked out a loop, a little less than two miles, and I did the loop. At first, I walked most of it. But as I went out night after night, I ran a little more and a little more.

Soon, I was losing weight. My body was craving foods that were better for me, although my diet still needed work. I was able to run more and more of the loop, with some setbacks, but it was generally two steps forward, one step back, so there was always forward progress. And I discovered, much to my joy and amazement, my stress was relieved and my brain used the time to ponder on the deep questions of life and existence that were shaking my identity. Running helped me tremendously.

Once I had lost the weight and my identity crisis was over, it was tempting to stop running. And for a brief moment, I did. But stress built back up, my brain needed the time to ponder and think on things, and so I went back out. Ever since then, for almost twenty years now, I've maintained the habit of running.

When life has been hard, running has often been the answer. My brain still uses that time to think through things, ponder questions, or sit with hard emotions. When life is good, running is no longer the answer but rather a discipline I maintain so that, when life gets hard, it can be the answer, the solution, the respite, to my problems again.

That's what discipline in life and faith is all about. Discipline means to be regular about our good habits, whatever they are. It's the root of the word disciple, what we all are to Christ. To be a disciple requires discipline, spiritual habits, that form us and keep us grounded in Christ. Then, when the storms of life come, those habits cause us to never be moved/shaken/terrorized.

And that discipline isn't a checklist of behaviors or morals. Even for those under the law in Torah, it wasn't a checklist of behaviors or morals. This list of eleven items is not a to-do list but rather evidence of a disciplined life lived with God. That's because we cannot exhibit these kinds of behaviors unless we are dwelling with Christ on a regular basis. We need God's grace to empower us to be kind, to do no evil, to not harm our neighbor, and to stand by our oath even when it hurts us. We need that grace on a regular basis.

But even more than that, when times are good and we're disciplined, we continue to go deeper into relationship with God. And it's that depth, of making consistent habit to dwell with God, that causes us to "never be moved/shaken/terrorized."

If we're not regular in our spiritual habits, we're not a disciple. Rather, we use Christ, like we use aspirin or church, for our own benefit. Which means we take advantage of God, the God to whom we owe everything, the God who created all things. Such is dishonoring of God, shows God no respect, and turns God into a divine medicine cabinet for all the aches and pains in life.

And then, when we are moved/shaken/terrorized, God somehow doesn't seem present. God seems far away. God doesn't seem to deliver. But why should we have that immediate experience of God's presence if we've spent the good times not present with God, far away from God, paying little attention to God? If that's been the case, when the darkness comes, we have to find our way back to God and that takes time. But if we've been with God all along, we already know how to find our way to God, how to take solace in God; discipline pays off in the darkness. It's like practicing fire drills; they teach us what to do so we can find our way instinctively in a fire.

That's the power of prayer. It makes that pathway to God. As we retrace that path, we learn to see it no matter the darkness. So long as we stay disciplined in prayer, we can always find our way to God.

I say that less out of theological conviction, and certainly not because I'm a pastor and I'm supposed to say that. I say it because it's true in my life. It used to be that I was like a yo-yo: disciplined with God when times were hard and undisciplined when times were good. I was even that way when I first became a pastor. But a sermon convinced me of the necessity of regular habit, and so I began one. And so I have found that, in my life, even the gravest of difficulties have not left me moved, shaken, or terrorized. I have known times of insecurity, but I've always been able to experience God's presence, God's provision, and God's abundant love, because I stayed disciplined in the good times.

It's like when the power went out one night at our house. A storm raged such that the only light in the house was when a flash of lightning struck. But in the laundry room, where I thought the flashlight was stored, there was absolutely no light because there were no windows. I grasped around the cabinet, trying to find the flashlight, but to no avail.

Jackson, my oldest son, knew just where the flashlight was. He'd been playing with it, but had always put it back where I'd left it: not in the laundry room but the pantry. He went into the pitch-black pantry and came back out with the flashlight, knowing exactly where it was.

That's what life is like in the darkness when we're disciplined in prayer during the good times. We know just where the flashlight is because we've been going to it over and over again before the darkness settled in. God is our light in the dark times. If we're good about going back to the light in prayer over and over again when times are good, if we maintain discipline, it's very easy to find the light when the darkness settles into our lives. And finding the light means we're safe, secure, unmoved, unshaken, unterrorized. But if we're not disciplined during the good times, we're like me in the laundry room, grasping blindly in the darkness for a light that turned out not to be there.

It's more important during times of stability to maintain a discipline of prayer than it is during the dark times. It's more important because then we know our way to the light when darkness comes. And then we experience the goodness and grace God has for us, empowering us to be more like this list of eleven traits. For the people of God are a wonderful, good people, when disciplined in prayer.

Commit yourself to be disciplined in prayer. If you don't know where to start, or if you look back on your life at a string of failed attempts to be spiritually disciplined, I have two pointers for you. First, you may be choosing the wrong form of prayer for your personality. Check out Appendix 1 for resources on different kinds of prayer, like Lectio Divina, meditation, and prayer journaling. Be willing to try them all. It's a wonderful thing to be experimental with ways of praying. See what practice causes you to feel connected to God. Second, go to church on a regular basis. There's no replacement for encountering God in community. It helps us stay focused and disciplined.

For discipline is more important when times are good than when times are bad. Maintain your disciplines to know the way to the light. Then you "shall never be moved."

# Chapter 4

## THE POWER OF REPETITION

### Scripture Reading: Matthew 6:5-15

Prayer teaches us to find our way back to God in the dark, especially when our prayer is routine. How do we establish such a routine? How do we find our way forward? That's where we go next, learning that repetition can be a key to that routine, to help us know the pathway of prayer all the better.

Let us begin.

My soul groaned the words, over and over again. *Gott, laß meine Gedanken sich sammeln zu dir. Bei dir ist das Licht, du vergißt mich nicht. Bei dir ist die Hilfe, bei dir ist die Geduld. Ich verstehe deine Wege nicht, aber du weißt den Weg für mich.*[1]

Over and over again, my soul brought these words to my mind. The longing, yearning, of my soul in a language other than my native tongue. I had learned the words, taken them to heart, and they had become a part of the language of my soul.

I was lost, unsure of what path to take or where I would even find a path to take. It was a dark time in my life, a crucial moment where I knew I was in the forge and I hoped the fire would refine rather than destroy. That was all I had at the moment: Hope. And so I prayed that simple prayer, here translated into English: God, let my thanks rise only to you. With you is the light. You do not forget me. You are helpful. You are patient. I do not understand your ways but you know the way for me.

That was the deep prayer of my soul, one it uttered over and over again: I do not understand your ways, but you know the way for me. It was less a prayer of confidence that such was true but rather a request: Let me see, let it be known in me, that you do in fact know the way for me; let me see that the fire of this forge will refine,

---

1. Taizé, "Aber du weißt den Weg für mich," *Music of Unity and Peace* (Berlin: Deutsche Grammophon, 2015).

not destroy.

My soul groaned. The words of old songs I learned long ago came back to me, the language of my soul. The words I had formed in my innermost parts through repetition and worship. The words of psalms, the words of the Taizé community, rang within me, tuning my soul to prayer.

My soul went back to what it knew. Such is the power of repetition as it puts the language of prayer into our bones. Perhaps that is what Jesus had in mind when he taught his disciples the Lord's Prayer found in the scripture reading for this chapter: for that simple yet profound prayer to get into their bones, becoming part of their makeup. For prayer is a groaning and longing of our soul. Prayer is the language of our heart, given to God. Our hearts gain that language through repetition, especially the repetitious reading of scripture.

Such was the case as I arrived at the top of a mountain, huffing and puffing, my lungs feeling the sting of the cold air, and saw the vista. All I could do, overtaken by the joy in my heart, was say, "I lift up my eyes to the mountains—where does my help come from? My help comes from the Lord, the Maker of heaven and earth" (Psalm 121:1 NIV). Psalm 121, in its entirety, resonated deep within my soul, causing my heart to offer praise to God.

But we have to come down from the mountain, and when we do, sometimes our souls groan a different psalm: "My tears have been my food day and night, while people say to me continually, 'Where is your God?'" (Psalm 42:3 NRSV). Then my soul remembers, "Deep calls unto deep at the noise of Your waterfalls" (Psalm 42:7 NKJV), as the depth of me cries out to God from the pain, challenge, or hopelessness of the "valley of the shadow of death" (Psalm 23:4).

And when we arrive back at the mountaintop, we recall the words of David in that same psalm, "The Lord is my shepherd, I shall not want." Indeed, when we find ourselves in that "valley of the shadow of death," we know we can "fear no evil, for you are with me. Your rod and Your staff, they comfort me." We all know these words, those of Psalm 23.

That's the power of repetition. Tracing and retracing the same words, the same meanings, gives our hearts the language to groan, yearn, and praise God from the depths of our souls.

That is the point of the prayer Jesus teaches the disciples. He gives them not instructions for formulating their own beautiful prayers with amazing words, lyrical patterns, and beauty that would astound anyone. No, he gives them a prayer to recite, to say over and over again to become the language of their souls.

Which might feel foreign. At Rotary Club, one of the members asked me why I say basically the same prayer over and over again to open our meetings. His inference was clear: I wasn't praying right if I repeated the same prayer time and time again.

Protestants can be averse to repetition, saying that there's no life in it, that somehow all prayers must be extemporaneous, off the cuff. Otherwise, how can it be straight from the heart?

Straight from the heart like: "As the deer longs for flowing streams, so my soul longs for you" (Psalm 42 NRSV), or "O give thanks to the Lord, for he is good, for his steadfast love endures forever. Let the redeemed of the Lord say so, those he redeemed from trouble" (Psalm 107:1-2 NRSV).

That's the challenge Jesus notes in his instructions: Pray straight from the heart. Don't be like those pompous people who construct beautiful prayers to impress others. They aren't praying to God but, rather, praying so other people can hear them pray. And that's not prayer. They aren't praying from the heart.

Don't be like the priests in the temple who like to hear themselves talk. If they pray so they can hear themselves and think they're big stuff, they aren't praying from the heart.

Don't be like those who put big, impressive words and constructs into their prayers, hoping to somehow manipulate or move God to action on their behalf. God can't be manipulated by our prayers. And such prayers aren't praying from the heart.

Underlying all of Jesus's "don't do it this way" comments is this: Prayer should be from the heart. It should be the language of the heart.

But rather than teach extemporaneous prayer, telling people how to pray off the cuff like that Rotary member, Jesus gives a formula, a prayer for repetition. In this repetitious prayer Jesus taught us, the one we call the Lord's Prayer, we find the foundation for our prayer lives. Indeed, it serves as the model prayer, teaching our souls how to pray and giving voice to our deepest longings.

First, it encompasses all the different kinds of prayer. Not every prayer must have all these elements, but prayer can have any of these elements:

Address to God (our Father)

Praise of God (hallowed be your name)

Submission to God's will (your kingdom come, your will be done, on earth as it is in heaven)

Petition for needs to be met (give us this day our daily bread)

Statement of humility (forgive us our trespasses)

Recognition of our humanity (as we forgive those who trespass against us)

Request for help (lead us not into temptation, but deliver us from evil)

Jesus shows us what prayer can encompass, what the fullness of prayer sounds like, and in doing so, this prayer becomes the foundational prayer for any other prayer we utter because any prayer we give comes from this prayer. Perhaps we are praising God; it is grounded in "hallowed be your name." Maybe we need help from trouble; "deliver us from evil" becomes the bedrock of that prayer. When facing a tough decision or time of discernment, our soul whispers, "your kingdom come, your will be done." The Lord's prayer encompasses all the different kinds of prayer we might utter.

And, secondly, the Lord's Prayer does something else far more powerful. Through repetition, the words get into our soul, giving voice to the depths of our spirits when our own voice fails. When we aren't sure what to do, our souls with yearning declare, "Your kingdom come, your will be done." When someone makes us angry and we need to forgive, the words "forgive us our trespasses as we forgive those who trespass against us" remind us of our common humanity, of how much we ourselves need to be forgiven, which becomes the fuel to forgive others. When we need to feel close to God, our souls cry out, "Abba," the informal, familiar, affectionate name for God, what we translate as "Father" in the Lord's Prayer.

The Lord's Prayer teaches our souls to cry out with the familiar words, giving our souls the language they need. When we say the words over and over again, they get deep into our soul. They become a part of who we are. They graft themselves onto our souls and shape and mold us. And so, when we come before God in prayer, those words become the bedrock, the base, of our prayer life. We cannot help but pray these words as our hearts yearn and groan in prayer. This is especially helpful when we do not know what to say, for the repetition gives our souls the vocabulary to cry out to God.

That's the power of repetition. Not that prayers cannot be extemporaneous, but even then our extemporaneous prayers are deepened, given new life, when they have words to pull from, language the soul and heart have gained through repetition.

While the scripture referenced at the start of the chapter is deep and robust with much to teach us, the main lesson I want to convey is this: Repetition gives our hearts the language of prayer, helping our souls cry out and find their way to God.

So it was for the ancients. Before literacy was common, those attending services would learn prayers through repetition, hearing them over and over again in the temple or church. The ancients designed the psalms to be just this way. They were the hymnbook of ancient Israel, sung repetitively, such that those attending temple services would know them by heart. That repetition creates the language of prayer; it teaches us instinctively how to find our way to God.

Every psalm I quoted here I recited from memory as I wrote. The psalms are the language of my heart, along with some Taizé music and hymns. They have gotten deep down in my soul so that, when a deep-seated emotion comes into my life, whether for good or bad, whether positive or negative, I experience the blessing of hearing my soul pray a psalm or hymn that fits the emotion. That recitation connects me to God in the powerful way only repetitious prayer can, for it leads my soul back down forgotten paths that lead to the peace and joy of Christ.

For example, in the midst of chaos, I hear myself say, "Praise the Lord, you sea monsters!" Psalm 148's take on the chaos of life, a reminder that God is in the midst of chaos, moving for order. When disaster strikes, I hear myself say, "We're marching to Zion,"[2] a line from a hymn that recalls Psalm 132, where the people march up Mount Zion to the temple, as they had done for years, but the temple in this case is destroyed. It's only rubble. In front of them is evidence that suggests God has been faithless. But the people refuse to believe that, defiantly marching up the hill anyway, declaring God's faithfulness. What a powerful witness! And my soul gives praise for that in the midst of disaster.

Repetition enlivens our prayers, gives our emotions voice, and lets our heart communicate more deeply and thoroughly with God. Repetition, even in worship, teaches our hearts to sing the praise of God, whether in familiar or foreign times, whether in joy or sorrow, whether in peace or fear.

Lord, teach us to pray. When those deep, hard, emotions of life come, do you have the words to pray? When there are inexpressible joys, when the depths of you cry out in pain, does your soul, does your heart, have the words it needs? If the answer is no, the power of repetition teaches our souls how to pray no matter how difficult, dark, or light the emotion is.

"Lord, teach us to pray" is a request not to learn how to petition God so that we can get what we want, but it is instead a request to learn how to communicate with God so that we can experience the fullness of who God is in our lives. It's a request for prayer to change us; for a robust communication channel between us and God. And the best way to learn is repetition so that our souls are formed by hearing the words of scripture, especially the Psalms, over and over again.

So here's my challenge to you. Read scripture or the Psalms daily (see Appendices 4 and 5). Say the Lord's Prayer daily. Develop a habit so that you gradually build your own soul bank of verses for your spirit to use when your soul yearns and groans for God. And when sitting to pray, follow the model set by the Lord's Prayer. (For reference, that model is included in Appendix 2.) In the Psalms, you'll learn to do what the Lord's Prayer teaches us: repetition, instilling the words of scripture deep in our hearts so that our hearts are enlivened in prayer.

That way, as you go through life with its ups and downs, twists and turns, joys and sorrows, your soul will always have the words to give praise, petition, demand, raise in anger, or utter deep joy. Let the Psalms, as with the Lord's Prayer, become the language of your soul. Practice repetitious prayer, just as Jesus taught us with the Lord's Prayer. Lord, teach us to pray.

---

2. Isaac Watts, "Marching to Zion," in *The United Methodist Hymnal* (Nashville: United Methodist Publishing House, 1989), 733.

# Chapter 5

## BRINGING OUT OUR MESSES

*Scripture Reading: Luke 3:1-6*

Repetition holds power for helping us find our way down the pathway of prayer, especially when life gets difficult. In those times of challenge, prayer requires our willingness to be open and honest about how we're feeling. Such authenticity is hard and incredibly risky, but for prayer to change us, we must be willing to bring out our messes.

Let us begin.

On the way back from a trip with our youth group, the director and I somehow got on the subject of the 1996 Olympic Games in Atlanta. It's possible she and I were at the same event, a baseball game, without knowing each other. But such was the case for the huge events held in the old Fulton County Stadium and in Centennial Olympic Stadium.

During the Olympics, I remember walking down the streets of Atlanta going to Olympic Stadium and to Centennial Olympic Park, and thinking how beautiful everything looked. The sidewalks were pristine. The roads were clear. Everything was picture perfect.

The same was true of Berry College, where I grew up. Berry hosted the Olympic Youth Camp, so we had young athletes from all over the world staying right there on campus. Berry looked the best I had ever seen it. Atlanta, Berry, indeed the whole state of Georgia had prepared itself for the advent of the Olympics; we had prepared the way for the athletes, the dignitaries, the visitors from all over the world.

Such is the case when we prepare ourselves for any event of significance. At the Christmas season, we prepare our homes for the advent of visitors, we prepare ourselves for the advent of Christmas parties as we dress our best, we prepare ourselves for the advent of Christmas Day, ensuring that we've purchased gifts for everyone on our list, that the house is ready, the breakfast casserole ready, the gifts wrapped. We labor hard to make sure we're prepared.

So prepare the way! That's the word from Luke in chapter 3 of his gospel. Prepare yourself for the advent of the Christ child. Prepare yourself for the arrival of the salvation of our God. Prepare the way of the Lord! Make straight his paths.

Back in the day of this chapter's scripture reading, the streets were largely unpaved. Reading descriptions of these roads often reminded me of the dirt roads in the rural county where I currently live. When I first got my convertible, I took it for drives all around the county, both to enjoy the car and wanting to get to know the county better. I have since stopped taking the car out and ride my bike instead. That's because my little car, with its ride close to the ground and low-profile tires, can't handle the bumps, the potholes, the sudden dips and rises. One day, I figured, I was going to get my car stuck or ruin a wheel.

Such is not a complaint; it's just the nature of dirt roads. And by comparison with the roads of ancient Palestine, the dirt roads of Dodge County are like a newly paved highway. Very often, ancient roads leading from town to town were winding affairs, fraught with potholes and bumps that could ruin your cart. Sometimes, the road simply ended because sand or storm had ruined part of the path, leaving travelers looking for where the road picked back up, hoping they were traveling in the right direction. All too often, the roads between cities, where there was not much traffic, were frequented by robbers and bandits who would rob and maul passersby.

And in the wilderness, in areas not frequently traveled, visitors encountered strange sights. They would hear the sounds of animals not previously known. Sometimes, they'd catch sight of animals that defied the imagination: gazelles, sand cats, striped hyenas, and oryx. These are crazy animals, they looked strange, and gave the wilderness a mythic quality. They'd also encounter the endless sands of the desert, the heat of the desert, all reasons to turn around.

For one only went into the wilderness if absolutely necessary. Today, travel through the desert parts of Jordan, Iraq, and Saudi Arabia, what our ancients called the wilderness, is possible because of modern roads but, back then, rarely did anyone venture into the wilderness. It was too wild, too foreign, too scary, too desolate, and too hot.

Rather, travelers would go up and around the desert, the wilderness, rather than go through it, like avoiding Atlanta or any major city by taking the long way around. To avoid the craziness, travelers went around on a much longer, but safer, cooler, and easier journey.

But not for the advent of God's salvation. John states that it will come through the wilderness, across the straight path made by raising up valleys and lowering the mountains. It will come from the place of chaos, the foreign place of heat, it will come through the rough ways made smooth. The advent of the salvation of God will come from the most unlikely of places.

The advent of the salvation of God would come through chaos, through mess, through trouble. The salvation of God would come not through the nicely kept streets and well-worn traveled ways, but rather through the hard, difficult, challenging places of chaos and fear. The salvation of God would come through the messes of existence.

And to that, John proclaims that the people must prepare. They must get ready. "Prepare the way of the Lord" is the constant refrain. But this is a far different preparation than we typically make for guests or Christmas. John declares they must bring out their messes to put on display.

To understand what he means, imagine with me that you know you have a house guest coming. If your house is like mine, with two children and a hectic pace of life, there's usually a mess. Dishes, no matter if they're done once a day, pile up in and around the sink. There are blankets strewn over couches. One day, I walked into the kitchen and found my path blocked by a gaming chair that had somehow been thrown into the walkway, yards away from its usual location. And my wife's favorite: My shoes usually end up wherever I kicked them off, and then wherever the kids have pushed them or the dog has taken them. The house usually has some sort of mess to it.

So imagine with me that, to prepare for the advent of a house guest, you leave the mess out. Not just that, you also go and find the messiest things you've hidden away: the gross drawers in a bathroom, the unkept closet full of junk, the food long forgotten in the back of the pantry or freezer. You pull all this out and put it on display, adding to the mess.

Outside, you make sure to throw leaves everywhere across your yard, one full of grass that is tall and untidy. The bushes have lots of uneven growth, and your trees are in need of water. In the back of the house, you have an old beat-up car you keep around. This car goes in front of the house, on display for all to see.

Then, finally, you put your dumpster on the side of the road, stacking bags of trash and boxes around it. Leaving the doors to your house open, now, with the trash out, the yard unkept, and messes presented around the house, you're ready for your house guest. You are prepared. You have prepared the way of the Lord, making straight his paths, as John has asked.

This is the kind of preparation John calls for. A straight path through the wild, the desolate, the messy things in our lives.

For this is what we do when we respond to the John's proclamation of a baptism of repentance for the forgiveness of sins. We put our messes out, we present our trash to God, making straight Christ's healing path through all of our brokenness.

The phrase "a baptism of repentance" might be better put this way: a cleansing of guilt. We are freed from the guilt of sin that comes too easily, and lingers too long, when we realize some sin in our lives. We are freed from regret of past actions. A cleansing of repentance is far different from a call to repentance, which is admission of guilt. Baptism is cleansing, and John offers freedom from the guilt, regret, and angst that too often accompany sin and the memory of sin.

For sins are forgiven. Sins meaning anything that has put separation between us and God. Sometimes this is something we do, and sometimes this is something done to us, something we can't let go of. Forgiveness is release—release from the oppression of our sins and the sins of others.

We all carry around those burdens, that brokenness, that mess and trash. We have old wounds that seem stubborn in their refusal to heal. We have secret sins we've failed to confess to anyone, and they eat away at our insides. We have sin, things that we know separate us from the love of God. And to that sin, John tells us that Jesus wants to cleanse it, forgive it. Thus the call: Prepare the way of the Lord! Make straight his paths through your burdens, brokenness, mess, and trash. Pull it all out. Place it on the side of the road. And allow Jesus into it.

Prayer is the vehicle for us to bring out our messes. At least, it can be. When we present an open, honest, description to God of all our trash, of the disgusting recesses of our souls, that kind of honesty opens the gates of our hearts to the healing grace of Christ.

It requires courage, but we can do it if we're brave, bold, willing to be vulnerable with our savior who offers healing in our lives. We can do it, or we can be like Tiberius, Pilate, Herod, Annas, and Caiaphas. I'm fascinated by the list at the start of this scripture. In this list of names are the villains of the story of Jesus's earthly ministry or, in the case of Tiberius, villain of the early Christian movement. They sought to stand in the way of Christ's earthly ministry. They heard the call to prepare and, rather than bring out their mess, they hardened their hearts. They would not let Jesus in. They put the mess away and closed the door.

They were like some houses off of rural roads: dark, far off the road, with no lights and with a big fence and gate to bar entry. No one should come visit, no one should dare enter, for there will be no visitors, no guests, no advent, so no preparation. They are guarded, seeking to be invisible. That's the heart of Tiberius, Pilate, Herod, Annas, and Caiaphas.

This morning, which describes you: the messy house or the dark house? Are the gates of your heart shut or wide open?

I suggest that too often we all put on a face, thus closing the gates of our heart. We're perhaps too afraid to admit that we have messes, that we're not as put together as we appear to be. I confess to you that I regularly need some healing in my life. I'm just as messy as everyone else. My heart gets hurt like everyone else. I sin like everyone else. I stand in need of healing, just as we all do.

So prepare yourself, present your messes for tidying, open the doors to your heart and present your messes. If you desire healing, if you need a cleansing of guilt or forgiveness of your sins, if you are shouldering burdens caused by the sins of others, there is one way and one way only to encounter the healing love of Christ: Prepare the way by bringing out the mess. Go to God in prayer, telling God about your messes. Put the trash of your heart out on display, bring out the hidden messes, and place them before Christ in prayer.

For, indeed, that is the "salvation of our God." If you need to be saved from yourself, from burdens, or from anything at all, pray, bring out your messes, and experience the healing of God's grace. It's hard, it requires tremendous courage, but it is the only path to healing.

Bring out your mess. Pray with emotional authenticity. Prepare the way of the Lord.

# Chapter 6

## AUTHENTIC PRAYER

*Scripture Reading: Psalm 137*

Sometimes, bringing out our messes means praying our anger or other harsh emotions to God. That's an incredible challenge because often we would rather hide those particular messes away, lest they overtake us or we be found out to be as angry or mean-spirited as we really are. And yet, authentic prayer demands that we pray everything to God, even the harshest, meanest, angriest of things.

Let us begin.

Every Fourth of July, somewhere, usually more than once, I hear a song that seems appropriate to the occasion. The chorus especially seems to speak to the birthday of the United States. The lyrics bespeak doves, reckoning by the weak over the strong, the triumph of the righteous, and call the day by the traditional name for our national holiday, Independence Day.

Sounds appropriate for the Fourth of July, except that the song has little to do with that occasion. The tale weaved through the verses tell a story of domestic abuse. The main character endures this abuse while the town looks the other way, leaving her feeling she has no option but to "stand by her man." Then, after years of enduring the trauma of abuse, she takes actions into her own hands in order to end the abuse.

Now that the abuse is over, the woman knows independence. The title of the track, that same name as our national holiday, refers to the day this woman was released from the abuse of her husband by burning down the house. Not only that, but the song leaves open the strong possibility that the abused spouse has murdered her husband by killing him in a house fire.

This is a hard song. It speaks of things not mentioned in polite conversation.

It goes to the depth of human experience that we might think is best left unsaid. When someone wrongs us, when someone hurts us terribly, when someone arouses within us a deep anger and hatred, we bury those things deep. These things are not to be spoken about. They're not to be mentioned. They're to be shoved away—try to forget, try to move on.

But we don't forget. Anger over the hurt and wounds we carry eats away at our souls like a cancer. Hatred infects us like a deadly disease. The harder we shove that anger and hatred into the recesses of our soul, the more it eats away at us from the inside out. We might not speak of it out loud, but inside, we're crying out for revenge, for justice, for vengeance.

Were we to speak out loud of this part of our experience, we would find great commonality. More of us than we would expect could speak to a deep anger or hatred. Very often, it comes from a family member who's done something terrible. Other times, it's a boss, former coworker, or a member of our church. Whoever the person, I bet all of us have known the kind of anger, the kind of hatred, that burns down deep inside, creating within us fantasies of getting revenge, of getting even, of doing something harmful back to the person who has harmed us. And at some point, should we have the courage, we must all admit that we have harmed others out of our anger, as well. We have been the recipient of deep wounds and the giver of the same.

Anger that drives us to hurt others is a common part of being human. It's true for all of us at times in life. And it was true in biblical times. That's the case in the Psalms. And because it was true in scripture, because scripture often gives voice to this silenced part of the human experience, we'll speak here of this unspeakable thing: anger that drives us toward committing harmful, wounding, vengeful acts of our own.

The psalm referenced for this chapter is not easy. It shares much in common with that difficult song about abuse, arson, and murder. So, because it speaks to what is not mentioned in polite conversation, let us approach it with an open mind, an open heart, and a willingness to engage. We must be willing to be honest with ourselves, for what God has in store for us through this psalm offers the power to relieve us of our anger and hatred. But we have to be willing to engage it. So, with lowered defenses and a willing spirit, I ask you to pause the reading of this chapter and read Psalm 137.

This is not an easy part of scripture. Some refer to it as a "text of terror," one of those parts of the Bible that speaks of unspeakable things. Here, we have the people of God, the chosen ones, the elite from the nation of Judah, telling God the thing that would make them happiest is infanticide: to murder Babylonian children.

It's all the more remarkable that the murder of children is where the psalm ends.

It doesn't try to spiritualize or justify its intent. It simply ends there. And it makes no apology for itself. The Israelites state how they feel: "God, here is what would make us the happiest. Here's what needs to happen to rectify the wrongs we've experienced. Here's what would restore balance and harmony. Inflict upon the Babylonians what they did to us. And not only that, but we want to murder their children so that their empire, their nation, dies off without a trace."

And let us remember, this is a prayer; a corporate prayer of the people of Israel. It's not simple poetry; it's a prayer to God, as all psalms are. Verse 7 directs the conversation about getting even directly to God: "Remember, O Lord, against the Edomites," which is another word for the Babylonians. Remember what they did! Remember their destruction! Remember how they murdered our people!

For those in exile, this memory is still vivid. They're only a few years out from watching the Babylonians sack Jerusalem. They destroyed the temple, which was bad enough. But then they went into the fields and destroyed the crops, sowing salt into the ground to make it uninhabitable. Then they burned the city, burned people's houses, raped women, and murdered children.

And in a coup de grace, they inflicted a cruel punishment upon their leadership. They took the King of Judah outside of the city while it burned, making him watch the destruction of his people and his city. They then lined up his sons in front of him. While he watched, they brutally murdered all of his sons. Once done, they plucked out the king's eyes so that his last visual memory was of the destruction of Jerusalem and the murder of his sons.

In warfare, the Babylonians were a cruel people. Knowing this, it becomes easier to justify the rage of the people of God. Of course they're looking for revenge! It's no wonder they're deeply angry and hate the Babylonians. Terrible, unspeakable things have happened to them.

And then, as the psalm tells us in verses 2-6, the Babylonians taunt them in captivity. The people are mourning, they're deeply depressed, but their captors taunt them, asking them to sing the songs from the temple, asking them to praise God. Of course the Babylonians have no desire to worship God; they simply want to humiliate the people. Even here, a few years after the destruction of Jerusalem, the Babylonians won't relent lording their destruction over their captives.

But even still, infanticide? We might empathize with their anger, even if we have never experienced anything like what they have. We might see how they could be justified in being deeply angry. But to prayerfully ask for infanticide? How can that be?

We speak, through poetry, about the unspeakable all the time, especially in our music. I imagine several of us have sung along to songs without realizing what, exactly, we were singing. Hip hop speaks to getting revenge with great frequency.

Country music talks about getting even. I've joked that the worst girlfriend in the world has to be Taylor Swift because so many of her hit songs are about how terrible her ex-boyfriend is. And one day, while singing along to a mid-'90s pop song, I realized the song, cheerful-sounding as it is, is really about covering up a grisly murder.

In our modern poetry, and here in this ancient poetry, we give voice to the voiceless, speak of the unspeakable, because what goes on in the dark recesses of our souls needs to be brought to the light.

That's the power of this kind of psalm and prayer like it. It brings to the light what lives in the darkness. Hatred is like mold: It loves a dark environment and shrinks before the light. In the dark, it will grow inside us without being seen until one day it's overtaken us and we're consumed by our anger and hatred. Such consumption looks like having fantasies about getting even, scheming to hurt someone, believing everyone is against you, thinking that no one really loves you, or just good old-fashioned anger about everything.

But when it's brought into the light, it shrinks away, and quickly. That's what this psalm does, and that's why it's important for us to learn to pray this way. If we're brave enough to admit that we have anger and hatred we're holding onto, we must be brave enough to bring it into God's light through prayer.

The light always ushers away the darkness. We must embrace the darkness, admitting its existence, so we can bring it to God in prayer. During difficult times, the darkness can be overwhelming, especially because it seems to come on suddenly, throwing the order of our times of stability into chaos. It's traumatic when that happens; it's destabilizing.

And it's tempting to stuff our feelings away, down deep, trying to avoid the darkness. But we can't. We have to embrace the darkness. Here, in the darkness of anger and hatred, we must do the same, in a particular and careful way.

For rarely does someone set out to harm someone else. Rarely does someone wake up one morning and decide that today is the day they're going to do their best to ruin someone's life. If they do, we call that psychosis: a psychological disorder.

For the vast majority of us, rather, we act in evil ways that hurt others because the anger has grown so large within us that it begins to control us. And that control causes us, almost thoughtlessly, to act vengefully. Like that mold, the anger grows within us such that it comes to control us. We hurt others with our words. We malign others by spreading falsehoods about them. We say terrible things online. Perhaps we even physically assault, but regardless, we look for opportunity to do some sort of damage to another person, the person we hate, because our anger has come to control us.

I have not been immune from such feelings. Familial relationships have led me to that kind of anger because of the way others have hurt me. When I've served in various leadership capacities, including as a pastor, almost inevitably someone hurts me, for this is part of the nature of being a leader. But even though I know being hurt comes with the territory, when that anger comes, an anger born of a wound inflicted by someone else, it's terrible. It impacts my home life, as I'm less present at home and have to take time away to tend to my soul. It impacts my health, as I feel the stress and sorrow of the wound inflicted. It impacts my soul, as the deepest wounds create doubt and lead me into the darkness.

And the way for me to not take revenge back, the way I have learned to cope, the way to not let someone else's anger that has wounded me cause me to turn around and wound them, is to bring my anger to the light.

That's what we all must do: bring our anger to the light. Anger, like mold, withers before the light of God. We find ourselves relieved, we find ourselves healed, we find ourselves forgiven, and we even find ourselves freed of the terrible burden that is the anger and hatred we carry around.

And to bring our anger to the light is simple: It's to pray like Psalm 137.

Our anger needs a release valve, but we tell ourselves over and over again that we're not supposed to feel that way, that it's wrong to feel that way, that we just need to forgive and move on, that we're a good Christian so we're not supposed to have these kinds of feelings. Or we want to cling to our anger, holding onto it, because that's the temptation of anger: to hold on such that it grows into rage and hatred.

And yet, we're also human, no matter how strong our faith is. Anger is a natural occurrence. Faith doesn't relieve us of ever being angry. No, faith grants us the means to handle our anger well. Things will happen to us that are terrible, inflicted upon us by someone else. And when that happens, the worst thing we can do is not tell God about it.

So tell God exactly how you feel. Tell God what you'd like to do to make things right, even if it sounds similar to the ending of this psalm. It might be that you strongly desire to do the wrong thing. That happens, it's human nature, and it's called temptation. And the best thing we can do with any temptation is tell God what we want to do.

For telling God what we want to do brings that terrible thing to the light. For me, the last time I got hurt my prayer sounded like this: "God, I've been grievously wronged. I'm angry and I'm scared. I'm confused. What do I do? I want to take revenge. I want to stand up and say what's right. I want the other person to know how hurt I am and I want to hurt them! God, help me." My prayer journal from that time has several pages with prayers like this.

And I share something this personal because I want you to know how universal it is to feel this way. We do ourselves much damage by telling ourselves we're not supposed to feel that way, that it's wrong that we feel that way. It's the actions born of feelings that are wrong. Feelings are sometimes temptation. We can't stop the feeling from coming. But we can be faithful in how we respond to that feeling.

And the way to be faithful with temptation, with hard, unspeakable, feelings, is to bring them to the light of God by turning them into prayer. Like in the last chapter, this is another way we pray with authenticity, for to be authentic in prayer requires bringing all our messes before God, even the ugliest, meanest, and angriest.

So do that. Anger, hatred, will shrink before God when we turn it into prayer. That's what this psalm shows us. So far as we know, the people of God never committed infanticide in Babylon. They never did anything to harm the Babylonians nor their children. They never took any action against them. Instead, they gave God their anger, shone the light of God on their hatred by taking it to God in prayer, keeping them from acting on temptation and healing them in their angry, broken places.

Live into the example of this ancient psalm. Give God your anger. Don't be ashamed of it; prayerfully give it up. Let God's light shine on it.

If you recognize anger in your life, if you can see where you've got hatred you've been holding onto, let God's light shine upon it. Admit it to God in prayer. Tell God exactly how you feel and exactly how you feel about the other person. If you've been tempted to do something harmful or inflict some sort of pain upon someone else, tell God about that, too. And if you've committed some harmful action that has hurt others, confess that and ask God for forgiveness. Let the light shine, for anger stands no chance against God's light. All we have to do is prayerfully bring it before God.

Pause now, even while reading, and pray with tremendous honesty. Pray, for God's light is shining down and will conquer even the most deeply-seated hatred. Pray, for the darkness of anger stands no chance in the light of God.

# Chapter 7

## PRAY WITHOUT CEASING

### *Scripture Reading: Acts 1:6-14*

When we have prayed with emotional authenticity, routinely treading the pathway of prayer over and over again, we discover we are not alone. Life can be lonely, but a regular routine of prayer makes it easier to find our way to the heart of God, back to our experience of God's presence, where we discover that we have never actually been alone.

Let us begin.

One of my first conscious memories is a song, "Stand By Me," by Ben E. King. I'm not sure why that particular song, I'm not sure where I picked it up exactly, but when I hear it, there's a deep resonance within my soul.

It pricks at something deep inside me, something that's uncomfortable. This isn't one of those fuzzy, nostalgic memories, but one that usually makes me change the song when it comes on. Weezer, a favorite band of mine, recently put out an album of covers, one of which includes "Stand By Me." I still haven't listened to the song all the way through; it's too uncomfortable.

This song pricks at a powerful motivation deep inside of me that has driven decisions and actions to provide for my family, to ensure that the future is secure for my children, and to reconcile and restore relationships. All those are good things, all things I feel are part of the mission God has given me on this earth, which helps partially explain why the song makes me uncomfortable. I feel the burden, the weight, of responsibility.

But beyond that, there's also a deep-seated fear, and perhaps you can relate: the fear of being alone.

I find resonances of that fear in the beginning of Acts. Near the start, Luke describes the moment Jesus ascended back to heaven. Almost in passing, we remember this moment in the Apostle's Creed. The creed includes a litany of Jesus's life with this line: "He ascended into heaven and sitteth at the right hand of God the Father Almighty." It's an easily missed reference to a significant event.

In the Christian calendar, we remember this moment on Ascension Sunday. This is not a day as high and holy as, say, Easter or Christmas or Good Friday. And yet, Ascension Sunday is a very important day in the life of the church—the day we remember that Christ returned to heaven, triumphant, in front of his disciples. He gave them a mission, the Great Commission of verse 8, that says, "You will be my witnesses in Jerusalem, in all Judea and Samaria, and to the end of the earth" (Acts 1:8). This, after telling them the Holy Spirit was coming, providing them the power to live out this mission. Then he leaves in a way reminiscent of Elijah (cf. 2 Kings 2:9-12).

But the main point is this: He left them. Like Elijah before him, he left his disciples. Elisha, after witnessing Elijah's triumphant rise to heaven on chariots of fire, then left, carrying Elijah's mantle, to take on Elijah's prophetic vocation. That's where the phrase "passing of the mantle" comes from: the mentor giving charge to the mentee, as happened with Elijah and Elisha, and just as Jesus did with his ascension.

And when that happens, it's up to the next generation, the next person, the mentee, Elisha, the disciples, to carry on the work.

I relate strongly to that. I feel that pressure that comes from things passed on to me, things I inherited. Some of them are things I would rather not have inherited but things that remain my problem anyway. I feel that pressure to go at it alone, because no one will do it for me, to live out the deep motivations I feel in this life, the deep things I take as my mission.

Perhaps you can relate. Maybe you know people in your life who are similarly driven. This is different from being driven by ambition for jobs or money or status. This is driven by things that are far deeper and more meaningful. For me, questions like, "Will my children be better off than me?" or "What wealth will I leave to them?" or "How's the emotional health of my family?" drive what I do. From lived experience, I am aware that no one will secure my family except me, no one will provide for them except me, no one will take care of them except me, and no one will do for me except me. I am alone as I live out that mission.

Just as no one will do for your families except you. Perhaps in the latter years of your life, you can look back and see how you did just that. Or maybe you look back with some layer of regret. If you're in a middle-aged generation, you see that older generation and either have an example of how you want to turn out or how you don't want to turn out. Perhaps at the start of your adult life, or in middle or high school, you looked forward to a life that you'd build with great expectation and a "sky's the limit" attitude.

Wherever we are in the stages of life, we know at a base level that no one will do things for us as we live out our lives. We are alone as we traverse the journey of life.

And no one will do for Elisha except Elisha as Elijah returns to heaven, passing the mantle. He is alone as he enters his prophetic ministry. Just as it seems the disciples are alone now, with Jesus having ascended to heaven

They are seemingly alone, just as we are prone to feel alone as we carry out the weight of the burdens we feel in this life. The mantle has been passed, the tasks inherited, and we move boldly forward into the future alone, for no one will do things for us.

Jesus leaves the disciples with the Great Commission of verse 8, one that Luke uses to structure his book. The book of Acts moves forward with receipt of the Holy Spirit and then the gospel spreading to Jerusalem, to Judea and Samaria, and then to the ends of the earth—in other words, the Gentile world. It's a beautiful literary device and leaves us with the impression of the spread of influence, something that has resonance for our lives today.

At another moment at the end of Jesus's ministry, in Matthew, Jesus gives a mission to his disciples. It's the more famous of the Great Commissions: "Go and make disciples of all nations, baptizing them in the name of the Father and of the Son and of the Holy Spirit" (Matthew 28:19 NIV) But unlike in Acts, Matthew records Jesus saying, right after giving the mission, "And surely I am with you always, to the very end of the age" (v. 20).

It's language very reminiscent of Psalm 23: Even though I walk through the darkest valley, I will fear no evil, for you are with me.

Throughout scripture, we hear this pledge from God: I am with you, always. In the garden, God is with Adam and Eve. Even after sinning and being banished from the garden, they still have God with them. God is guiding the generations that followed, through Abraham, through Joseph, through Moses and Joshua and David and the kings and the prophets, including Elisha.

On an intellectual level, we know this. God was with the disciples, God was with Jesus, and God remained with them even after the ascension. God has always been with humanity, and God is always near at hand for us to search and find. God wants to be found and wants to be in relationship with us because God loves us unconditionally.

We are never truly alone. And we know that.

So why do we feel so alone?

It's easy, on mountaintops, to experience God. At the top of Wigington Road, just north of Walhalla, South Carolina, is the most beautiful vista I have ever seen from an Appalachian mountaintop. I've seen similar from the Blue Ridge Parkway in North Carolina and Virginia, but this one takes the cake for me. From up there, you can see seemingly forever, for there's no obstruction as you look south-southeast. You can see two deep blue mountain reservoirs, the Town of Walhalla, and many other sights to discover. It's simply breathtaking.

From any vista like that, it's easy to feel close to God. These are the literal mountaintop experiences of life, and they're much like our metaphorical mountaintop experiences: We feel close to God, all is right in the world, and we do not feel alone.

But eventually, we come down from the mountain. We cannot stay there forever, whether looking at a vista or coming down into the hardships of life from our metaphorical mountaintop experiences. Here, the disciples gather on Mount Olivet, where they witness Jesus rising back to heaven. After he is gone and the angels dismiss them, they walk down the mountain.

What they couldn't have known as they entered the upper room, down in the valley, is all the hardship that was to come. A chapter later in Acts, there will be a metaphorical mountaintop experience as they receive the Holy Spirit, but then they will discover trials, persecution, death, shipwreck, ostracism, and a whole host of the hardships that are to be found in the valleys of life. The book of Acts spends the vast majority of its time in the valley after opening on the mountaintop.

It would be tempting for these early disciples and the early church they founded to feel alone. But they don't. Even before they have received the Holy Spirit, during this moment as they enter the upper room with other disciples gathered there, both men and women, they do not feel alone.

The Holy Spirit is the presence of Jesus Christ with us always, God's gift and fulfillment of Jesus's promise to be with us always. But here, even in the days between the Ascension and Pentecost when Jesus is gone and the Holy Spirit has not yet arrived, the disciples do not feel alone.

How? Jesus is gone, but they don't feel alone. How do they not feel alone? The answer lies in the phrase from Acts 1: They "devoted themselves to prayer."

So why do we feel so alone? Because we are not devoted to prayer. And by prayer, I do not just mean sitting, head bowed, eyes closed, talking to Jesus. Prayer is more about posture and less about talking. Prayer is attuning ourselves to God, to the Holy Spirit that is the presence of God with us always. Prayer happens when we garden, when we walk, when we work, when we feast, when we cry, when we hurt, when we drive, when we rejoice, when we do anything in life that is not sin, if we are attuned to God in that moment.

For prayer means being centered in God, no matter what activities we engage in.

Luke tells us that the disciples were devoted to prayer, constantly praying. It's unrealistic to think the disciples were constantly praying the way we do when we talk to God in our head or listen along with someone praying out loud. This is how we tend to conceive prayer. Paul calls on disciples at the church in Thessalonica to pray without ceasing. To do so the way we conceive of prayer would be to do nothing else in our lives. That, of course, is unrealistic.

But that's not what's meant by prayer. To pray is to simply take a moment to be with God's presence in our lives, no matter our activity. Because God is always there, always with us, no matter how alone we feel. The question is whether or not we are aware of God's presence with us. And the way we become aware—for it's human nature to lose that awareness—is through prayer.

Prayer means being centered in God, no matter what activities we engage in.

We do not pray enough, which is to say we do not take the time to make ourselves aware of God's presence with us. Prayer is about reorienting our spirits back to their true home, in the heart of Christ. All our cares and concerns take us away from that central home, that center, that space where we know, without a shadow of a doubt, that we are not alone.

The disciples in that upper room knew that even before the Holy Spirit had arrived. It was no matter that Jesus had gone back to heaven. They were not alone.

Neither are we.

And when we become aware of God's presence through prayer, we discover that the heavy loads we carry, the things that drive us on a very deep level, the challenges we face, the hardships we endure, the things that make us angry at the way things turned out, all of those things are much easier because prayer causes us to know that Jesus's "yoke is easy" and his "burden is light" (Matthew 11:30).

These earliest disciples knew that. They had the weight of the mission, the Great Commission, that Jesus had just given them. They knew they had quite a task in front of them as they moved to found the church. They must have known that the mountaintop would yield a valley experience, perhaps for a long time. That certainly could have come with great weight, with crushing burden, to not let Jesus down. But Luke tells us they simply devoted themselves to prayer; they knew that the yoke of their mission was easy and its burden light because they were devoted to prayer.

Prayer means being centered in God, discovering that Jesus carries our burdens with us, moving in power to accomplish the missions he has given us.

What burdens are you carrying today? What deep-seated motivations drive you, making you think that no one will do for you, that you must do it yourself? Too often I am pushing myself hard, whether for my family or for my church, because I believe no one else will do it for me and it must be done. But that's not the attitude of prayer. That's the attitude of self-centeredness rather than God-centeredness. That's the attitude that "I can do it all by myself and I don't need anyone's help."

The irony is that the missions God has given us in this life are things we decide we'll live out on our own. Here's what I mean: I believe God has called me to do some significant work for my family. And then I decide that I will go about accomplishing that work on my own, even though it's a God-given mission that God wants to accomplish through me by God's power! All I need to do is pray and act out of the wisdom that comes through that prayer, but instead I decide that I'll go my own way and make it work. When I do so, the work is hard, and it wears me down. Such leads to loneliness. Such leads frequently to feeling rundown, defeated, and exhausted because I've decided I can do it without the tremendous power of the Holy Spirit that is available to me always.

For if I take time to pray, the yoke of that mission becomes easy and the burden of these deep motivations becomes light. Prayer changes us by making our burdens and yokes light.

I wonder, can you relate?

We don't need to go at it alone. Whatever deep things we feel, whatever regrets might be attached to them, the missions we feel, the callings, the things we want to accomplish for ourselves, our families and loved ones, the legacies we want to leave behind, these are most likely things God wants for us. We find out if they are, and the burden of accomplishing them is lifted, when we take them to God constantly in prayer.

So go to God constantly in prayer by centering yourself in God, taking the time to make sure that, in every task you do and in every moment of the day, you are attuned to God's presence with us. For all the things we carry in life, pray without ceasing:

When you're at work and feeling exhausted, pray.

When you're at home and feeling overcome, pray.

When you're walking and thinking through your cares and concerns, pray.

When you're grieving, pray.

When you're gardening, pray.

When you're digging a hole, pray.

When you're donating money, pray.

When you're paying your bills, pray.

When you're fighting again with your relative, pray.

When you're feasting, pray.

When you're hungry, pray.

When you're full of joy, pray.

When you're angry at the way things turned out, pray.

When you're cooking, pray.

When you're trying to heal a broken relationship, pray.

When you're chatting with a dear friend, pray.

When you're fixing that stupid thing again, pray.
When you're delighted by something you own, pray.
When you're driving, pray.
When you're living, pray.
Stop. Pray. Without ceasing. Give thanks in everything.

For God is with us, always, even to the ends of the earth, even to the ends of the age, even to the ends of ourselves. God labors with us. God comes alongside us. God lifts our yokes and burdens and makes them light when we pray.

John Wesley, on his deathbed, is quoted as saying, "The best of all is, God is with us."[1]

Do you know that? When do you pray? How often?

You are not alone.

---

1. James Harrison Rigg, *The Living Wesley* (London: Charles H. Kelly, 1891), 214.

# Part 2: Prayer Changes Us

# Chapter 8

## LEARNING TO HEAR GOD'S VOICE

*Scripture Reading: Acts 9:1-19a*

How do we distinguish God speaking to us from all the other voices in our heads? This is the ultimate reason to pray regularly and with authenticity: to learn God's voice. All the previous chapters have led to this point, for we ultimately want to hear God speak so that we can know how to do God's will and how God is calling upon us to be molded and shaped, to be changed. That's the power of authentic, repetitious, without ceasing prayer; it changes us by attuning us to the voice of God, where we hear the calling of God and feel a deeper awareness of his presence.

From this chapter forward, we will learn how prayer changes us by making us more holy, just as God is holy. We begin by learning to distinguish God's voice from all the competing voices and noises in our daily lives.

Let us begin.

For my family, May 24 is a very special day every year for it is our oldest son's birthday.

Back in 2019, I was in Washington, D.C. Jackson, my oldest, had asked to go on a trip with me to celebrate his ninth birthday. We saw the House and Senate chambers, the White House, the National Art Gallery, the dinosaurs, the planes at the Air and Space Museum, and the thing that had Jackson the most excited: the International Spy Museum. It was a trip to remember.

May 24 is also a special day in Methodism. In seminary, I learned that May 24 is Aldersgate Day, to celebrate John Wesley's special encounter with God on Aldersgate Street in London. It's debatable whether or not he was converted, saved, or just had a special encounter with God, but on May 24, 1738, Wesley reported that his heart was "strangely warmed," and he felt an assurance of his salvation. For years, Wesley worried about whether or not he was really saved. No matter how hard he disciplined himself, he would still sin. The presence of that sin made him anxious that, perhaps, he wasn't really saved.

But here, at the home of an acquaintance, he felt that assurance. It came while someone read the introduction to Martin Luther's commentary on the book of Romans, a dry read if there ever was one. And yet, in the middle of this academic, rote study, Wesley's heart was "strangely warmed," and from that day on, his life was changed. He rarely questioned his salvation moving forward and, from this seminal experience, gave us our theology of grace that pervades all we do as Methodists.

God spoke to Wesley that day, just as God speaks to the apostle Paul, previously known as Saul, on the road to Damascus in Acts, the scripture reading for this chapter.

This is one of the most famous scriptures in the Bible. Everyone knows of this moment, where Saul encounters Jesus. And, indeed, it's a powerful moment. Jesus comes with "light from heaven," flashing, and a voice that speaks directly to him. Colleagues traveling with him hear the voice, too. It's an incredible moment.

It reminds me of stories from the Old Testament. God comes to Moses on Mount Sinai with flashes of light and a voice from heaven. Isaiah sees an incredible vision and hears the voice of God when he is called to be a prophet. There are similar encounters throughout the Old Testament where God speaks directly to someone he has called.

Just like here. Saul is God's chosen instrument, a new kind of prophet who will bring the good news to the Gentiles. His travel companions witness this incredible moment, a moment so amazing they are rendered speechless. God has spoken!

Wouldn't it be great if God spoke to all of us that way? Most of the time, we're left scratching our heads wondering if God is speaking to us at all. Wouldn't it be great if we had the kind of clarity that comes with flashes of light and a voice from heaven? Wouldn't it be great if we had our own Damascus Road experience?

I've heard that phrase used often by churchgoing folks when they speak of trying to discern if God is talking to them. They wish they had a "Damascus Road" experience. Or they talk of their salvation, feeling a certain awareness of it but wishing they knew for sure, as Saul knows for sure here, that God has forgiven and saved him, echoing John Wesley before his Aldersgate moment. I've even heard pastors say they wish they'd had a "Damascus Road" experience when speaking of their call to ministry. They wish they had that kind of assurance when the road gets tough.

Wouldn't it be great if we did have that kind of encounter? Our own Damascus Road or Aldersgate moment? Then we'd know for sure it was the voice of God.

And that's the thing. We want to discern the voice of God. We know God speaks, sometimes directly to us. How are we to know the voice of God? How are we to know that God is speaking? God doesn't seem to grant Damascus Road experiences often, so how are we to discern the voice so we will know what is the will of God, "his good, pleasing and perfect will" (Romans 12:2 NIV)?

I get that question a lot. People ask me, "How do I know God's voice? How do I tell if it's God speaking? How do I know the will of God?" As Saul, turned Paul, says in Romans, how do I "test and approve what God's will is" (Romans 12:2 NIV)?

It's not simply a big theological question for academic debate. There's room for that, such as asking why God doesn't grant theophanies to everyone, with theophany being the big theological word for sensory encounters with God. And yet, why we aren't all granted theophanies is a practical question, too. When we're making a big decision like, for example, whether or not to take a job offer, it sure would be nice if we had a theophany, a Damascus Road experience, to know what God would have us do. When deciding how to care for a loved one: whether or not that person should move into our home or go to managed care or a treatment center, a theophany would be hugely helpful.

Instead, whenever there are decisions—big and small—that we take to God in prayer, we most often seem to encounter silence or a bunch of different voices in our heads, and we struggle to sort out which one, if any, are God. When deciding how best to parent, when deciding if we should quit a job, when deciding how to manage our money, when deciding anything of significance, a theophany would sure be helpful. So, why is it that God doesn't come in a visible way to all of us?

It's in decision-making that we usually seek to listen for God's voice. But note that such is not the case here. Saul wasn't seeking to make a decision; he'd already decided to go and seek out Christians, "breathing threats and murder." He'd made up his mind. There was no decision to make. Rather, Saul's life is dramatically interrupted by the voice and light of Christ on the road to Damascus. Saul gets a theophany.

And then there's Ananias, who's home minding his own business, not seeking to make any decisions, when he receives a vision from God. This word "vision" could mean hearing a voice, having a sense, or actually seeing something, but I suspect it's hearing a voice because he hears God say to "get up and go to Straight Street." Ananias hears a voice, just like we want to when we're faced with decisions, but note that the voice doesn't come through in flashes of light nor from heaven. Ananias hears without the spectacular aspects of Paul's theophany.

This is much like the experience of Elijah in 1 Kings 19, where he, too, heard what 1 Kings calls a still, small voice. It's not with thunder, lightning, whirling trees, or any other visible presence of God. It's a still, small voice that speaks. It tells Elijah to return and face his fears, and it tells Ananias to go and face his own—confront the most hated man among Christians, bringing him into The Way, as Christianity was then called.

And then, while he's waiting, God's voice has been speaking to Saul, although perhaps not with words. Saul expects Ananias to come, but it's not clear that God is actually speaking with voice. Perhaps, Saul knows that someone is coming, has that conviction of confidence, like John Wesley when his heart was strangely warmed. He is simply aware, senses God's presence, and knows he will be taken care of.

So here, within this one scripture, we have three different ways that God speaks: with a visible presence to Saul, with a voice to Ananias, and with a sense of confidence with Saul as he awaits Ananias. Three different theophanies.

Add to this that God speaks in a variety of different ways throughout scripture. In Daniel, a hand writes on a wall. To Elisha, there's a chariot of fire. To Elizabeth, Mary's cousin, there's a leap of her baby in her womb. For the Israelites trekking through the wilderness, there's a column of fire by night and a cloud by day. To Samuel, God calls his name.

God speaks differently throughout scripture. But one thing is clear: the people who hear from God know with confidence that it is God and respond accordingly. And that's the central question for us: How do we hear from God with confidence? When we have decisions to make or we just need to hear from God—to hear a word of comfort, to hear and have assurance that God is with us, to feel assured of our own salvation—how do we hear from God with confidence?

We can be assured that God does speak to us in ways we can comprehend with confidence, because God loves us and desires relationship with us. God wants to be heard. There's no doubt in my mind that God speaks to us in ways we can understand. God speaks differently because we are different people. And God will always speak to us in a way we can understand.

Consider the examples we've looked at so far. On the Damascus Road, God speaks to Saul in a way that he can understand. He approaches Saul just as he has approached prophets in the Old Testament. Saul, being a Pharisee, would know those stories well, so coming through a theophany, a visible presence, would speak Saul's language. And then, the presence of witnesses confirms the story. In Deuteronomy, two unrelated witnesses are required to validate any story and make it credible, something Saul would know well (Deut. 19:15). That is exactly what occurs on the road. God comes to Saul with a theophany not because Saul is special, but because that's how Saul will understand him.

Just as the still, small voice to Ananias comes in a way that works for Ananias. When he hears the voice, he simply responds like the prophet Samuel who heard the same voice by saying, "Here I am" (1 Sam. 3:4 NIV). Ananias knows the voice because God has revealed that voice to Ananias.

To Saul, awaiting Ananias's visit on Straight Street, God comes with presence, one that Saul is able to recognize. This is not unlike John Wesley having his heart strangely warmed at that house on Aldersgate Street.

To all of us, God speaks in a way we can understand. I testify to you that I have experienced God speaking to me many times, and I always know it's God. I cannot explain to you how I know; I just know. I liken it to that scripture I alluded to earlier when we asked the question, "How do we 'discern what is the will of God—what is good and acceptable and perfect?'" The answer to that question is the fullness of that same scripture. Paul, writing in Romans 12, says: "I appeal to you therefore, brothers and sisters, by the mercies of God, to present your bodies as a living sacrifice, holy and acceptable to God, which is your spiritual worship. Do not be conformed to this world, but be transformed by the renewing of your minds, so that you may discern what is the will of God—what is good and acceptable and perfect" (Rom. 12:1-2 NRSV).

If we are disciplined and authentic in our prayer lives, as we've discussed in previous chapters, we are being transformed by the renewing of our minds. It's that renewal that will cause us to discern God's voice. Our souls are tuned to God's heart. We grow in holiness, as discussed in chapter 2, which grows us in being more aware of God. Or more simply put, as the psalmist says, our deep calls to God's deep (Ps. 42:7), and in that calling, we hear back from God.

So the question is not whether or not God speaks. God does, with frequency. The question is not whether or not God is comprehensible when speaking to us. God is; God will speak to us in a way we can understand. God is speaking. God wants to be heard. The question is whether or not we're positioned to hear.

I submit that if we cannot discern the voice of God, it's probably for one of two reasons. First, there's no regular routine of prayer in your life. I am sure you have heard this many times from the pulpit, in Bible studies, and in Sunday school classes, but if you do not spend time regularly with God engaging in prayer, then it will be very difficult to discern the voice of God from all the competing voices that run rampant in our heads. There's no substitute for regular prayer, for it is by that practice that we "present [our] bodies as living sacrifice," and thus are "transformed by the renewing of [our mind]," as Paul says (Rom. 12:1-2). While there are extraordinary moments where God breaks into our lives, for the most part, if you want to know what God is saying to you, you have to spend time with God on a regular basis, in the good times as well as the bad, as discussed in previous chapters.

This is yet another way repetitious prayer in particular is helpful.

Then, when engaged in that regular practice of prayer, we will know the peace that passes understanding when there's no rational reason to experience peace. Then, we can experience joy even in hard times of life. Then, we will know hope when there's only reason for despair. Then, we will know love even when there's nothing but hate in our lives. Then, we will experience the powerful presence of God that can do the impossible, holding us close, making us know that, as St. Julian of Norwich famously put it, "All will be well, and all manner of things will be well."

And beyond that, we will hear direction from God, just as Ananias did and Saul did while waiting. God has called us to not only experience the blessings of relationship, but to go and share those blessings with the world. We are blessed to be a blessing. And God speaks to us still, just as God spoke to Ananias, so that we can go and offer ourselves as blessings to the world. That's the power of hearing God's voice, of experiencing God. And that's the first point: To know what God is saying to you, you have to spend time with God in prayer.

Second, I think too often we want to hear from God because we want God to make a decision for us. So we listen to all the competing voices in our heads, assuming one of them must be God. Sometimes in life, none of them are. God gave us freedom to make decisions; that's part of free will.

If we're spending time with God in prayer and we know what it is to hear from God and yet, in the midst of a decision, we do not sense a word from God, then make the best decision you know how to make. That's what Paul means by being "transformed by the renewing of your minds, so that you may discern what is the will of God—what is good and acceptable and perfect" (Romans 12:2 NRSV). Be bold, be brave, and be courageous. God gave us freedom for a reason and blesses our decision-making when the decision is left for us. Don't use a lack of a word from God as justification to be cowardly in decision-making.

Similarly, we shouldn't go to God looking for divine guidance in decision-making if we aren't going to God on a regular basis for worship and prayer. God is not only a divine guide for life, nor is God only to be used when life gets hard. God gave us everything; to only seek God when we need God is to use God for our purposes, a form of idolatry.

While God does sometimes break into our lives, most of the time, we don't hear from God because we're not spiritually disciplined. God speaks to us in ways we can comprehend. That's because God desires relationship with us! We don't need to have a theophany, a Damascus Road experience, because God will come to us in a way we can understand. The question is whether or not we're positioned to hear. In other words, you know it's God speaking when you've spent time seeking after God, when you've been praying regularly.

This is the point of all that's come before so far in this book. Regular, routine, disciplined prayer that's authentic even to our messes and hardest emotions is what teaches us to distinguish God's voice from all the others. Without routine, it will be much more difficult. Use the appendices at the back, if you haven't already, to find a prayer practice that you can keep. This practice of routine, repetitious, and authentic prayer is what paves the pathway of prayer for us, connecting us more directly with the heart of God. Then, we will know God's voice.

In knowing God's voice, we are changed into better, soldier people. We more easily exude the fruits of the Spirit, we more often follow God's ways, and we are fearless in decision-making. Distinguishing God's voice is the beginning of being changed by prayer. Such ability to discern comes through regular, repetitious, authentic, unceasing prayer.

Are you spending time with God regularly? I cannot stress enough how important that is for many reasons, but in particular, for being able to discern God's voice. God is there, God is speaking, and the question is whether or not we have ears to hear.

So I, with the apostle Paul, "Appeal to you therefore, brothers and sisters, by the mercies of God, to present your bodies as a living sacrifice, holy and acceptable to God, which is your spiritual worship. Do not be conformed to this world, but be transformed by the renewing of your minds, so that you may discern what is the will of God—what is good and acceptable and perfect" (Rom. 12:1-2).

Pray and you, too, will hear God speak to you that "good, acceptable, and perfect will." Then we will be changed for good.

# Chapter 9

## BECOMING SELF-AWARE HEALERS

### *Scripture Reading: Romans 12:1-8*

Hearing God speak changes us, making us better people. In particular, the regular practice of prayer changes us into self-aware people who offer healing to the world. That's the power of prayer when we engage regularly and the first example of the ways prayer changes us.

Let us begin.

Around us today is the social phenomenon of "cancel culture." On social media, if you encounter someone who upsets you, who says things that drive you crazy, who pushes your buttons, you can unfollow, defriend, or block them. Cancel culture takes that into the real world: When someone upsets you, unfollow, defriend, or block them by acting like they don't exist.

Take, for example, if someone says something that another person takes as racist. The first person says she didn't mean it that way and might even apologize. But because the second person is offended, he decides to "cancel" her, to act like she doesn't exist, to never engage with her again. That's an example of cancel culture.

In doing so, there's no chance for reconciliation, no chance for mutual understanding, and no chance for peace. There is, instead, the very denial of the humanity of the other, a cruel and fierce punishment.

Before we're tempted to say "it's others who act this way," let's consider how we all have lived into cancel culture without having called it that. There are family members we no longer speak to because of a history of hurt. In effect, we have cancelled them. There are friends we no longer have because the relationship fell apart over offense. We have cancelled each other. There are conflicts that have occurred, single conflicts even, between people that have led to no longer talking, no longer being on speaking terms. That's cancel culture, even though we wouldn't call it that.

We ourselves are well acquainted with cancel culture. It's a culture we would rarely feel we need, and very rarely consider engaging in, if we took Paul's advice from Romans: "Be transformed by the renewing of your minds" (Rom. 12:2), as mentioned in the previous chapter of this book. It comes from a very famous scripture reading, the one linked to this chapter. I'm sure you've heard it many times. Growing up, especially in youth group, I heard it all the time.

And when I heard it, the focus was always on sacrifice: Present your bodies as a living sacrifice. Don't be conformed to this world, meaning give up worldly pleasures.

Less discussed, if ever, was Paul's call to be transformed by the renewing of your minds. It's a call in equal measure to offering ourselves as sacrifices, and it's the antidote to conforming to the patterns of this world. Those three—offering, transformation, and nonconformance—are all linked together.

But what does that mean? What does it look like, to be transformed by the renewing of our minds?

Part of my discipline, my self-sacrifice, is personal study. This is beyond study related to sermons or teaching or church leadership; it's what I do for me and my relationship with God. That's been a habit for a long time. And lately, I've been reading about the Enneagram.

Among my peers, the Enneagram has gained much popularity. It's an ancient system of understanding different kinds of people in the world, who are identified by numbers one to nine. I initially dismissed it as yet another personality inventory, and I'm really over those. I've done every kind imaginable and I never found any of them particularly helpful.

But the Enneagram I have discovered is different. It's spiritual first, not psychological. It's from and still grounded in Christianity, not the social sciences. Among hip, new wave, evangelical churches in the suburbs, among my peers in The United Methodist Church, in mainline and in Catholic churches, it's gained quite a following.

Its power is in helping us understand ourselves not from the perspective of our best, which is what most personality inventories do. It, instead, does the very uncomfortable thing of considering us from our sin and wounds, from the ways in which our personalities lead us to be unhealthy and spread that unhealthiness to others. But here's the kicker: by unhealthy, the Enneagram means how most of us often tend to be.

Consider this: "Unhealthy eights are preoccupied with the idea that they are going to be betrayed. Suspicious and slow to trust others, they resort to revenge when wronged. They believe they can change reality, and they make their own rules and expect others to follow them. Eights in this space destroy as much as they create, believing the world is a place where people are objects to be used and contributions from others have little or no lasting value."[1]

As I'm an eight on the Enneagram, that describes me when I am unhealthy and what was once my natural state. It remains the place to which I return when life gets more stressful than usual.

It's tough to admit that we can often be so terrible, as I just described myself, but it is powerful, transformative, when we do. We all have unhealthy selves. And unchecked, if we go about life without being self-aware, without examining ourselves, we simply live life in this unhealthy state. We hurt people, we destroy relationships, we cause damage. We might find our lives are often characterized by drama. And when drama comes, we blame others for it, unable to admit to our own unhealthiness.

As the old adage says, "Hurting people hurt people." The problem often is too many of us are hurting and don't know it, but we act out of that hurt anyway. That's the definition of lacking in self-awareness.

And that's what Paul means. What does it mean, what does it look like, to be transformed by the renewing of our minds? The Enneagram holds a great answer to this question: It means to become a self-aware person.

So often when there is conflict, the issue at hand is complicated by unhealthy people acting out of their unhealthy selves. For example, a family finds itself no longer fighting over an inheritance or a surprising revelation or some other thing. Instead, the family is fighting out old wounds without even knowing it. The family members at odds act out of their hurt, their unhealthy selves, while claiming to be healthy and on the high ground in the argument. Eventually, the only outcome left is permanent division—cancelling each other, as we described earlier.

Paul says transformation of the conflict would come if each person involved could pause, see their wounds and how those wounds are driving the conflict, ask God for healing, and then come back to the table. The Enneagram concurs. It sounds simple, but we know it to be so hard.

So often, we have known this reality: Conflict brings stress. Stress brings on our unhealthy selves. Unhealthy selves cause us to create drama, which can cause relationship loss. Which brings more conflict. Then more stress. And the repetitive spiral continues as we, along with many others, continue to hurt people because we are hurting, because we lack self-awareness.

This is the normal state of affairs because we're all sinful, wounded, hurting crea-

---

Ian Morgan Cron and Suzanne Stabile, *The Road Back to You: An Enneagram Journey to Self-Discovery* (Downers Grove, IL: InterVarsity Press, 2016), 41-42.

tures with malformations in our personalities. Hurting people hurt people.

Consider these examples of unhealthy personalities:

You feel so busy and burdened by all the ways you're helping people, but when asked if you need help you dismiss the help, even feeling insulted that someone would ask you if you need help. But then you get bitter because no one will help you. This is an unhealthy two.[2]

When things are stressful in life, you get perfectionistic, insistent that all things are done, done well, and you can't rest until it's done. You drive other people in your life crazy as you do so while beating yourself up for not being good enough. This is an unhealthy one.[3]

If things get hard, you retract from life, refuse to engage with the difficulties of life, and retreat into things that bring you joy. You shut out the outside world, to the detriment of those who love you the most. This is an unhealthy five.[4]

During stressful times, you struggle to make decisions, turn to unhealthy behaviors like drinking too much or other things you know you shouldn't do, but you do it anyway so that you can feel some pleasure. This is an unhealthy seven.[5]

I'm sure we can all relate to one or more of those. We all have personalities that are ultimately grounded in sin and wounds. All of these describe people who act out of their wounds without knowing it. That means, they describe people in need of healing. Admitting that we have wounds in need of healing is the first step toward being transformed by the renewing of our minds.

And the next step? That's the challenge of the rest of our lives. To go to God in regular prayer to engage in one of the hardest things of all in life: Self-reflection. Why? Because a self-reflecting person is a self-aware person, a person who has been transformed by the renewing of his or her mind, a healthy person.

Self-aware people are rare but powerful people. Consider the difference in my type, eight, when it's healthy. We just read how, in my unhealthy state, where we all begin, I destroy things, I'm brash and difficult with people, I'm suspicious and actively protecting myself against betrayal that's more often perceived than of real.

When I'm healthy, when my mind has been transformed, when I'm self-aware, here's how I am, "Healthy eights are great friends, exceptional leaders and champion of those who cannot fight on their own behalf. They have the intelligence, courage and stamina to do what others say can't be done. They have learned to use power in the right measure at the right times, and they are capable of collaborating and valuing the contributions of others. They understand vulnerability and even embrace it

2. Cron and Stabile, 112.
3. Cron and Stabile, 91.
4. Cron and Stabile, 168-169.
5. Cron and Stabile, 207.

at times."[6]

Such a massive difference. And what makes the difference is the "renewal of our minds." It's self-awareness. Such comes through self-reflection. As we find sin and wounds, we present those to God for healing through prayer. We work through the ugly sides of ourselves, we push through pain, so that God can heal us. This is the journey to self-awareness, to being healthy. Then we will be transformed by the renewing of our minds.

Then we will be, instead of a hurting person who hurts others, a healthy person who heals others. That's the transformation to which Paul calls us; a transformation to a self-aware person.

Do you engage in self-reflection? When stressed, when hurting, when struggling, when there's drama in your life, do you ask yourself what role you played in it? Do you ask yourself how you contributed to it? Do you seek to understand better the complexities of your soul to know why you take offense or get hurt by certain things?

Self-reflection begins in prayer. When we tell God exactly how we are feeling and then prayerfully examine our motivations, we are being transformed by a prayer life that renews our minds. For God through love can hold up a mirror that reveals simultaneously who we are and who God has designed us to be.

John Wesley understood the importance of self-reflection for the transformation of our selves. He had twenty-two questions that he and members of his Holy Club would ask themselves each day in private to self-reflect. (These are included in Appendix 3.) Taking on this habit is a powerful way to be transformed by the renewing of our minds so that we can be healthy people who transform the world.

So here's the challenge moving forward: Practice the spiritual discipline of self-reflection via prayer. There are two steps to that. First, get a journal. Start journaling as an act of prayer. (See Appendix 1 for a few tips on this practice.) It's helpful to write the answers to the questions that you'll ask yourself. It may only be a crutch until you can get used to it in your head, but it's very helpful when beginning, especially if we are unskilled in the area of self-reflection. And I say unskilled on purpose, for it's a skill that requires cultivation like any other.

I have kept a prayer journal since 2004. For me, it has become the crucial tool in my prayer life to becoming more self-aware. At times, it makes me aware of wounds. Other times, I am able to work out issues related to those wounds and find healing. Always, because it's prayer, it presents me as I am, wounds and all, before God. Then I am changed. Prayer journaling changes me by offering healing and creating self-awareness.

6. Cron and Stabile, 41.

Second, use John Wesley's twenty-two questions for daily self-examination. Talk about them with someone close in life, with whom you can walk the journey to self-awareness. Most of all, talk to God about your answers through prayer. You'll discover things you never knew about yourself. Some of those will be very difficult. Very, very difficult. One of the hardest, if not the hardest, thing about self-reflection is admitting to ourselves the ugly side of our selfhood. We all have ugly sides. And those ugly, unhealthy sides drive us much more than we would like to admit. This is also something we can do in our prayer journals.

But here's the truth of the matter. And I say this as one who is still on the journey to self-awareness, but also as one who has found much healing because of this now many year journey: I am much better, much happier, much more confident, and have much less drama in my life because of that hard work, because I have found my ugly side, wrestled with it, and given it to God for healing.

That ugly side still exists. But when I come face-to-face with it, I know that my duty is to seek transformation through the renewal of my mind, to go to God in prayer for healing. I go and journal. I take time for me, to do things that encourage health in my life: running, bike riding, reading for pleasure, hiking or otherwise getting out in nature, and getting extra sleep. And while doing all those things, I ask myself the hard questions. I self-reflect. I pray and ask God to reveal the truth about my inner nature: where I am in need of healing, where sin is driving me, so that I can become a better disciple, so that I can continue to move toward self-awareness. In that time of prayer, as I am honest and self-emptying, there's healing from experiencing God's grace.

I engage in this challenging way because I know the power that comes when I act as a healthy eight, the healthy side of my personality. I build things, I accomplish things on behalf of others that were thought impossible, I inspire people, and I'm a leader that others can follow. And people find the healing power of the Spirit through me.

I want more days like that in my life. Not because it's pleasureful, but because I know that, when I'm healthy, when I'm self-aware, God can do far more than I could ask or imagine through me. And because I know that, when I'm unhealthy, I destroy things.

People who are not self-aware hurt others and destroy things. They cause drama and experience much drama.

People who are self-aware heal others and build things. They cause peace and experience much peace.

Hurting people hurt people. Healthy people heal people.

It's that simple.

Changing from one to the other comes through prayer, especially prayer that examines our wounds and ugly sides.

Which one are you?

Or do you even know?

Prayer changes us into self-aware, healthy, people. Commit yourself to the discipline of self-reflection through prayer. Be transformed by the renewing of your minds.

# Chapter 10

## FEAR INTO FAITH

*Scripture Reading: Habakkuk 1:1-4, 2:1-4, 3:16-19a*

Self-awareness developed by prayer will often cause us to confront our fears. When we are fearful, or discover fear we have harbored in our hearts, what do we do with that fear? How do we bring it to God in prayer? God wants to change that fear into faith, changing our what ifs into even ifs.

Let us begin.

There is a classic song by Bob Dylan, "All Along the Watchtower." Listen or search the lyrics if you can. If you didn't know better, you would think Habakkuk composed those words.

But they are Dylan's. Both he and Habakkuk see a world that feels "like a joke," full of falsehood and fakery. There's no reason to get excited because there's no relief to be had from the injustice of the world. So keep a watch in your watchtower, they say, and see the coming dangers, the coming violence, the coming injustice and oppression, while the rest of the world occupies itself with wine, pleasures, and falsehoods.

That indeed is where Habakkuk dwells in the biblical book that bears his name as he awaits God's action all along his watchtower.

Actually, not really. Habakkuk says he waits. But all along his watchtower, while he says he's waiting, he issues his complaint to God. The Babylonians are coming, there's danger lurking around the corner, and no one else is paying attention. They're too busy seeking pleasure. What are you doing about it, God?

In fact, upon on the ramparts, Habakkuk looks across the landscape and sees nothing but chaos, danger, and wrongdoing. So he says the law has become slack; he says that justice never prevails; he notes that the wicked surround the righteous. He sees a world marked by violence, injustice, oppression, and hatred.

Funny how relevant scripture can be.

How many generations of people have thought the world was going to pieces all around them? Habakkuk prophesied some 2,500 years ago thinking the world was coming to an end. So have people continued to think since. That's a lot of time in which people have been thinking to themselves that the world is coming undone. For certainly, each generation has had moments where it appeared that way.

And today, it's easy to look at the world Habakkuk saw of desolation, violence, destruction, instability, and wickedness, and see our own. If we go up in our watchtower and look out at the world, what do we see?

Across the world, at the time of this writing, we continue to emerge from the COVID-19 pandemic. From our watchtower, we see a world ravaged by a deadly disease struggling to get itself back to usual operation. The economic consequences hit the United States and Europe especially as supply chain and labor issues create inflation and other economic woes.

The refugee crisis continues because of terrible violence, although at a slower rate, as people flee their homes looking for safe harbor in a foreign country. Imagine what that would be like for us: leaving everything behind because life has become so terrible here that the only option left is to go to another country to find a home. Syria, Iraq, Algeria, Tunisia, and other countries around the Mediterranean basin continue to give up their citizens because of war-torn regions or miserable local conditions.

In sub-Saharan Africa, Muslims and Christians continue to kill each other. Ebola remains a threat. Unstable governments give way to rival tribes that fight, taking the lives of innocent people along the way and providing safe harbor for terrorist organizations like Boko Haram.

In the Middle East, tensions remain high across those varied international relationships. Iran and Saudi Arabia's rivalry spreads into places like Yemen, Iraq remains unstable, Syria remains on fire, and all the while Israel's politics are in turmoil as they struggle to find a unity government.

In Kashmir, the Hindu-nationalist Indian government and army occupy a once autonomous region, raising the specter of conflict, even nuclear conflict, with Pakistan who seems bent on defending the Muslim majority who live in that disputed region.

And of course tensions remain high across East Asia in Hong Kong, where protestors continue to fight with police and the Chinese regime; where China continues to seize land as it seeks to exert dominant influence over ocean waters; where the Koreas remain in their dangerous dance; and where rising ocean waters increasingly threaten and move villages in countries like Tonga.

All along our watchtower, we see a world that we want to work together to ad-

dress some of our greatest crises, like dangerous disputed regions, terrible killer dis-
eases, refugee crises, trade wars, global warming, and disastrous regimes. Yet when we
go and look from our post in the watchtower, we see nothing but reason for despair.

Indeed, we see the violence, the turmoil, the law that has become slack, the injustice, the strife and contention, and we cry out, "How long? Save us!"

What are we to do about it?

Habakkuk decides he will keep a watch to see if God will respond. But why?
Why keep a watch when you know what you will find? As Dylan notes, life is a joke,
there's no way out, there's far too much confusion. There's no relief, no justice, no
law, no righteousness to be had as we look out from our watchtower. Rather, there's
anxiety and fear of what might become of us and our world.

And so we ask ourselves, what if the world keeps burning? What if the world
never stops its injustice? What if these conflicts around the world escalate into terrible, even nuclear, warfare? What if our enemies attack us? What if the violence of
our society escalates? What if?

What if, God? That's our prayer all along our watchtower. We point to things in
our prayers and say just like Habakkuk: "Look! See the violence. See the injustice.
See the devastation."

Devastation indeed. That's perhaps the main thing Habakkuk sees. He notes the
violence and chaos of lawlessness, which cause him to tremble from within, cause
his lips to quiver, cause his steps to tremble beneath him. Habakkuk is scared. He is
fearful. And with good reason. Just look at the world! Just look at the devastation!

Habakkuk is fearful. And so are we.

Dylan's words written fifty years ago ring true today, just as Habakkuk's
2,500-year-old words do. We cry violence! And seem to get no word back. We see
two riders approaching in the night, but no one seems to be paying attention.

It's easy to feel like Habakkuk at the start of his prophecy: The law is slack, justice
never prevails, and chaos reigns. We, too, can keep a watch, but what's the point? As
Dylan aptly noted, it's a joke.

What if the world keeps burning? What if the world never stops its injustice?
What if these conflicts around the world escalate into terrible, even nuclear, warfare?
What if our enemies attack us? What if the violence of our society escalates? What if?

What if that's the wrong question?

Hear that same litany again, but asked differently.

Even if the world keeps burning, even if the world never stops its injustice, even if
these conflicts around the world escalate into terrible, even nuclear, warfare, even if
our enemies attack us, even if the violence of our society escalates, even if . . .

"I will fear no evil; your rod and your staff, they comfort me" (Ps. 23).

"Yet I will rejoice in the Lord; I will exult in the God of my salvation. God, the

Lord, is my strength; he makes my feet like the feet of a deer, and makes me tread upon the heights" (Hab. 3:18-19a NRSV).

Habakkuk begins with a million what ifs. But by the end, having taken his what ifs to God in prayer, God transforms his "what ifs" to "even ifs." That's the power of going to God in prayer. God turns the "what if" of fear into the "even if" of faith.

This is the message Habakkuk receives up on the ramparts. As he walks and waits all along his watchtower, he sees and hears God give this message of hope. And that message of hope is this: God turns the what if of fear into the even if of faith.

Hope born of knowing he serves a God who will strike out against injustice, oppression, and violence. In God's own time, God will move against his enemies. In Habakkuk, God tells the prophet the Babylonians are his tool for now, but the day will come when he will act against the Babylonians to protect Israel, when justice will prevail.

All along the watchtower, Habakkuk can envision the future when God moves in strength to undo the wickedness of the world. And so he can say, in the crucial verse of the entire book, "the righteous live by their faith" (Hab. 2:4 NRSV).

A faith that says no matter the fear that ensues, we will pray, "Even if, you are still God." Habakkuk gives us that witness. Even considering all the turmoil, violence, and reason for fear, the very last thing he says in his prophecy is this:

> Though the fig tree does not blossom, and no fruit is on the vines;
> though the produce of the olive fails and the fields yield no food;
> though the flock is cut off from the fold and there is no herd in the stalls,
> yet I will rejoice in the Lord; I will exult in the God of my salvation
> (Hab. 3:17-18 NRSV).

Can you hear Habakkuk saying, "even if"? This is the profound "yet" of faith. It's a yet that says no matter what I face, yet I still believe.

The righteous will live by faith, Habakkuk tells us, a faith that says in the midst of all the terrible reports we receive and see from our watchtowers, a faith that says when we see or encounter injustice, violence, oppression, and devastation, yet. ...

Yet I will worship my God
Yet I will rely upon the strength of my God
Yet I will rejoice in the God who created everything
Yet I will trust in the God who is among us still
Yet I will rely upon the God who is always moving for justice
Yet—the profound yet of faith.

All along his watchtower, Habakkuk discovers this powerful truth. The profound "yet" of faith allows the righteous to live by faith, allows the righteous to look out from their watchtowers, see the violence and injustice and then say, "Yet."

God will act. God will provide. And when we pray our worries and fears to God, our what ifs are transformed into even ifs. Thus we can pray with Habakkuk even if the worst happens, yet "I will rejoice in the Lord" who is the salvation of the world.

Here's the challenge. Karl Barth is famous for saying that we are to hold the newspaper in one hand and the Bible in the other. So, however you get your news, take in that news and then turn to Habakkuk, praying to God the profound yet of faith; a prayer that might sound like this, a prayer relevant for the time of this writing:

> Even if inflation rises further,
> Even if COVID-19 surges again,
> Even if the refugee crisis worsens,
> Even if India and Pakistan go to war over Kashmir,
> Even if religious wars continue unabated in Africa,
> Yet, I will rejoice in the Lord, I will exult in the God of my salvation.

The prayer of the righteous sounds like taking the news headline, praying it to God, and then adding at the end, "yet you, God, are strong and will save us." This is how we can have faith no matter what we see from our watchtowers. This is how the righteous live by faith.

Prayer changes us from a people of fear to a people of faith when we pray "even if" instead of "what if," when we pray with the profound yet of faith.

God is our salvation. God will save us because God is saving us, right now. Praying the profound yet of faith, even as we walk all along our watchtowers, will transform our eyes and ears to see and hear how God is moving and working in the world.

Take the challenge. Pray the profound yet of faith. The world is burning, yet "God, the Lord, is [our] strength" (Hab. 3:19a NRSV).

# Chapter 11

## BUT IF NOT: THE PRAYER OF THE FAITHFUL

*Scripture Reading: Daniel 3:19-30*

As prayer grows our faith through self-awareness and overcoming our fears, we experience God's call to mission. We are all members of the kingdom of God, called to Christ's mission to spread the good news to everyone we know. This requires that we are willing to cede our desires, needs, and wants to God. Prayer changes us into a people who can authentically pray, "Not my will but yours be done."

Let us begin.

A man walked down a trail along a steep cliffside. He'd come to enjoy nature, to enjoy the outdoors, to recenter himself. Life had been stressful as of late. His job worked him hard, and he constantly struggled against the unethical behavior of others, trying to do the right thing and set the example. He was known at work as a righteous man.

Which is exactly what he did at home. There, he was known, too, as a righteous man, always doing and saying the right thing. He loved his wife, he loved his children, he cared for them and they knew it.

In his community, he was known as an upstanding citizen, someone everyone respected. Many committees and boards sought after his presence. Sometimes, the more unethical of those boards would get frustrated with his Boy Scout ways, because this man always maintained his integrity.

He was hiking that day because it was his spiritual practice, for faith mattered a great deal to him. Indeed, he was an upstanding member of his church. Faith defined his identity, for he saw himself first and foremost as a brother of Christ, a son of God, a disciple. This was the basis of his integrity.

*85*

As he walked along, he came to a bridge that spanned a chasm between cliffs. It was a beautiful sight. Looking either direction, he could see for miles. The sun shone brightly but the air had a crisp feeling to it: the perfect day for a hike. He moved onto the bridge and paused to take in the scenery.

While he was there, another man happened to pass by. At first, their passing was a just a wave and a friendly "hello" until the passerby asked the man to hold onto his rope. It was a simple request and so the man obliged.

He took the end of the rope and heard the passerby say "thanks!" Then, suddenly, there was a huge tug on the rope, and the man was almost pulled off his feet. He dug in his heels, grabbed the rope with both hands, and, with great difficulty, got steady.

He held one end of a now very heavy rope. And as he followed the rope forward, he noticed it went over the side of the bridge. Carefully, steadily, with his heels dug in, he walked toward the edge of the bridge. Looking over, he saw the passerby hanging from the other end.

He yelled, "What happened?"

The passerby simply replied, "Just hold on!"

That was bewildering. Just hold on? This man had jumped off a bridge, with a huge drop below. If he let go of the rope, this man would certainly die.

"Climb up!"

"I can't; I'm too weak! Just hold on!"

"I'll pull you up. Hold on." The man grunted and pulled with all his might, but he couldn't pull the rope up high enough. It was simply too long and he wasn't strong enough.

So the man thought to himself that he could tie the rope to the edge of the bridge and then go and get help. Now that was an idea!

As he went to tie a good knot, his hands slipped and he barely maintained control of the rope. Tying the knot required that he let go a little bit with one hand so he could manipulate the rope into the knot. But the man was simply too heavy, the pull on the rope too hard, for him to do that.

And so he was stuck. Stuck holding a rope with a man on the end. If he let go of the rope, the man would surely die. He yelled for help but all he heard was the echo of his own voice. He was just stuck.[1]

Have you ever found yourself like this man: stuck in an impossible situation?

Have you ever been holding onto a huge weight, unable to let go of it, unable to get rid of it, unable to pull it up, just stuck?

Have you ever done the right thing and suffered the consequences of it? As the old adage goes, no good deed goes unpunished.

---

1. Paraphrase of Edwin H. Friedman, "The Bridge," in *Friedman's Fables* (New York: Guilford Press, 1990), 9-13.

Have you ever found yourself like his man, in an impossible situation because you did the right thing?

Here, in this story, is an example of that. Another example is found in the book of Daniel, the scripture reading for this chapter. That reading places us in ancient Babylon, with King Nebuchadnezzar demanding that everyone in the kingdom worship a new statue to a god he has set up. This new statue will be the focal point of all the kingdom's worship because the king has decreed it so.

But he has a secret motivation. He's captured the best and brightest of the society of Judah, which he has conquered. From Jerusalem, he took the intelligentsia, and here in Babylon, he wants them to contribute to Babylonian society.

It's a smart move. Take the priests and the doctors and the lawyers and the scribes and the philosophers and the prophets and the university professors, and make them a part of your society. They have something to teach you that you do not know; they have ways they can make your kingdom better.

The trick to this plan is assimilation. After immigration, these new people must be assimilated into Babylonian culture. Chief among the ways of assimilation is the worship of Babylonian gods, giving up worship of the gods of your homeland. But Shadrach, Meshach, and Abednego, high officials in the Babylonian government but Judahites by birth, refuse to give up worshipping their God, Yahweh.

This infuriates Nebuchadnezzar. He has promoted these three men above other, Babylonian-born officials. He has given them every advantage, hoping that if he won them over, he would win over all the Judahites in exile in Babylon. Their refusal to assimilate to his religion, to enter the melting pot of Babylonian society, stokes the fire of his anger.

Literally.

After all he's done for them, how dare they refuse him? He threatens to put them into a furnace, one that will certainly kill them.

And so, Shadrach, Meshach, and Abednego find themselves on a bridge, holding a rope with a man dangling at the other end. They are in an impossible situation: violate their fidelity to God and worship this idol Nebuchadnezzar has erected, thereby saving their lives, or willingly go to their death as martyrs for God. They're holding the rope with a heavy weight at the other end. What do they do?

We know what they do. This is a very famous story indeed. They set up a showdown of the gods: the erected golden idol and the god-king Nebuchadnezzar versus Yahweh. Nebuchadnezzar believes he has the power over his kingdom, including over religion. Yahweh proves him wrong by saving the men in the furnace, including sending an angel to be with them. They're so untouched by the fire that the scripture says not even their clothes nor hair smelled of smoke! This from the same fire that killed the guards who threw the three Judahites in there. It's incredible.

But that's not the most incredible thing to me in the story. The incredible thing is what they do with the weight on the end of the rope—how they handle their impossible situation.

On the bridge, the man knows he is stuck. And all because he did the right thing. He's left with prayer. And what should he pray? "God, get me out of this" or "God, send someone to deliver me"?

Before the king, as he threatens to send Shadrach, Meshach, and Abednego to their fiery deaths, what should these three pray? "God, get us out of this" or "God, send someone to deliver us"?

What do we pray? How do we seek after God in impossible situations?

For I am sure we can relate to the man on the bridge. We, too, have found ourselves caught up in an impossible situation because we did the right thing. We have known the old adage that "no good deed goes unpunished." We have provided over and over again for our families only to be rejected by our children or parents. We have pointed out corruption or unethical behavior at work only to find ourselves the one who is being punished. We have raised and loved our children to the best of our ability only to be rejected by them when they reach adulthood. We have invested our money wisely, prudently, only to watch it evaporate. We have done all the right things with budgeting our money, we have given faithfully to the church, and yet we still just barely get by. We have taken care of our bodies, only to find ourselves diagnosed with cancer. We have climbed the ladder at work, doing all the right things for our careers, only to find ourselves overlooked and under-appreciated.

We find ourselves in impossible situations all the time. We are holding the rope, with a huge weight dangling on the other end, unable to do anything except hold on.

Why would God allow for that to happen to us? We've been righteous, after all, just like Shadrach, Meshach, and Abednego. We've done the right thing, gone in the right directions, been righteous, maintained our integrity. We are the picture of an upstanding citizen and member of our church, just like the man on a hike who ends up holding this rope. And yet, we're just like him: on a bridge, holding a rope with a heavy weight on the other end, in an impossible situation.

It's very unfair.

Like Job before us, we might cry out to God to speak to how unfair this is. We might tell God that God hasn't come through for us like we've come through for God, and thus God owes us something. The balance sheet between us and God is out of balance, with our debits exceeding God's credits. It's time for God to step up!

We might do that. And that's therapeutic. In pastoral care, in counseling, I often recommend telling God exactly how you feel, just like in the chapter Authentic Prayer. God wants to hear those kind of prayers. God wants us to be completely auhentic, open and honest emotionally, in our prayer life, just as discussed in previous chapters.

And after we have emptied ourselves, after we have given over our emotional state and feelings to God, we still find ourselves on the bridge holding the rope before the king, facing the fiery furnace. We're still in the impossible situation. That's the hard part. We can find relief from our anger and resentment and bitterness through a robust, honest, prayer life, but it doesn't change the impossible situation in which we find ourselves.

So most of the time, we pray asking God to provide for us. We have a specific outcome in mind: deliverance, relief, release, resolution of conflict, restoration of relationship, more money, more time, more love, less pain. We pray for that specific outcome.

In the midst of an impossible situation, that makes sense. And we believe that God will provide that outcome we envision. We believe it with all our hearts. We hold onto it for dear life.

C.S. Lewis speaks to just that when referencing this scripture in a letter to Mrs. D. Jessup on March 26, 1954. Lewis says, "Two men had to cross a dangerous bridge. The first convinced himself that it would bear them, and called this conviction faith. The second said, 'Whether it breaks or holds, whether I die here or somewhere else, I am equally in God's good hands.' And the bridge did break and they were both killed, and the second man's faith was not disappointed and the first man's was."[2]

The faith of Lewis's second man is exactly the kind of faith that Shadrach, Meshach, and Abednego show. Look carefully at verses 17 and 18. These three say, in response to the king, "If our God whom we serve is able to deliver us from the furnace of blazing fire and out of your hand, O king, let him deliver us. But if not, be it known to you, O king, that we will not serve your gods and we will not worship the golden statue that you have set up" (Dan. 3:17-18 NRSV). But if not, whether we live or die, we are equally in God's good hands.

They are not convinced that God will save them. They are not convinced that God will come through for them in that way. All they know is that their duty is to be faithful to God, to demonstrate fidelity. If God doesn't save them, they still believe that they have done the right thing. Their faith isn't based on God coming through for their desired outcome. Note that they don't ask for deliverance or help, like we might expect. They're in a serious situation! And yet, they remain faithful, knowing that whether they live or die, they are equally in God's good hands.

C.S. Lewis, "Letter to Mrs. D. Jessup, March 26, 1944," in *The C.S. Lewis Bible* (New York: HarperOne, 2010), 58.

While it's okay to ask for desired outcomes and be authentic with God by sharing what we want, true faith doesn't rest on God doing exactly what we want. True faith prays for what we want and then says, "But if not," knowing that regardless of outcome, we are equally in God's good hands.

Shadrach, Meshach, and Abednego demonstrate true faith, one born of believing in the mission rather than in believing that God will always provide for you as you want.

That's a hard thing to swallow. It's hard for me to write. But this thing we call our faith, this relationship we have with Christ, this discipleship path we're on, the church we attend, isn't solely about having a better life. It's definitely not about having a social club. It's not about learning how to get what we want, even if what we want is very good and righteous.

Faith is, at its core, about ceding to God's mission in the world: what we call the kingdom of God. God is moving and working to bring about that kingdom. We are called to participate in that work. That's why we do the righteous thing, that's why we maintain our integrity, that's why we make sure that we do the right thing, because we are participating in God's mission for the world.

We are part of making the kingdom of God a reality on this earth or, as a famous 1980s rock song said, making heaven a place on earth, a place where love comes first.

That's what we are to be about. Faith means living out that mission into the world. To move ourselves toward being missional, we must learn to pray, sharing our desires and needs, but then willing to say "but if not," believing that regardless of outcome, we are equally in God's good hands. Prayer changes us by teaching us to cede outcomes to God, knowing we are always in good hands.

Sometimes, we will find ourselves in impossible situations. I cannot explain to you why that happens except to say that sometimes we are caught up between good and evil. For all our best efforts, for all our good discipleship, it still happens.

Sometimes, we will be on the bridge, holding a rope with a weight at the end, and have no recourse, nothing we can do about it.

Sometimes, we're in impossible situations. And in those situations, faith is this: trusting that you are in God's good hands no matter what the outcome is. Faith, true faith, doesn't rely on God to give us the outcome we decide we want. That's false faith, one born of self-centeredness.

True faith simply maintains fidelity to God, maintains allegiance, remains faithful to God and to the mission of the kingdom no matter how impossible the situation, without fear of the outcome. And to gain such faith, we pray, "But if not."

Does your faith rely on specific outcomes?

Or does your faith say that, whatever happens, you're in God's good hands?

Are you fully bought into the mission? Or are you fully bought into needing God to do for you whatever you think is best?

Here's another way to ask that question: Does your faith cause you to pray that God gives you what you want? Or does your faith cause you to pray, "Thy will be done on earth as it is in heaven"?

Paul tells us we were bought at a price. We are not our own. When we come to faith, when we become a Christian, we join a larger mission, a larger purpose, and we cede ourselves to that purpose. We are God's to be utilized as God sees fit.

What weights are you holding today?

What bridges are you on?

Are you facing an adversary like Shadrach, Meshach, and Abednego?

Pray, tell God exactly how you feel, be emotionally honest with God, and don't be afraid to ask for specific outcomes. But then pray, "But if not." Learn the faith of these three, believing that you are part of a larger work, you are part of the mission, the kingdom of God, and God is using you, even in the midst of an impossible situation, to make that kingdom a reality. Prayer changes us into fearless missioners of God's kingdom.

If you believe that, then you can say, whatever happens and no matter the impossible situations of life, "whether I die here or somewhere else, I am equally in God's good hands."

# Chapter 12

## SEEING THE WORLD AS GOD DOES

### *Scripture Reading: John 17:6-26*

P rayer changes how we see the world. Through becoming more self-aware, through ceding our fears, desires, and outcomes to God, we come to learn how God sees the world. This allows us to see beyond the divisions that characterize our lives, recognizing the divine image that lies within all of us. Prayer changes us by granting us the vision to see the world as one.

Let us begin.

We live in a time of deep division.

Perhaps nothing so starkly paints that picture than our politics. All the coverage points to our division as it speaks of Republicans, Democrats, conservatives, and liberals—a picture of how we are pitted against each other. Rather than philosophical disagreements, the two sides are portrayed as enemies of each other and sometimes enemies of the country. Our political parties are "us versus them."

Then there are other divisions, too. We paint ourselves in a rural-urban divide. We color ourselves into different groups through race and gender. We ask ourselves who the real Americans are, which is another way of saying what all these divisions say: the world is "us versus them."

Us versus them. It comes through loud and clear in our country and in our world. It's our farmers versus farmers in other countries, an underpinning of the trade war. It's our manufacturers versus China's. It's our way of life versus North Korea's. The world is us versus them.

Us versus them. It's the standard of our lives today. It's the favorite way for the media to portray our world. And we buy into it, both consciously and subconsciously.

And while we might like to ask what we are to do about it, as if us versus them were a problem, Jesus's prayer in John 17 sounds like us versus them. Perhaps Jesus sees the world in an us versus them lens, too? In this famous prayer in the garden before he is handed over to be executed, Jesus is very concerned about the disciples existing in the world. The world, in this prayer, sounds like the "them" of us versus them.

The world does not know the Father, so Jesus tells us. The world tends to reject the Father when it hears the gospel message. It runs the messenger out. It shows hatred and animosity. So Jesus asks God to protect the disciples: protect them from the world, from the evil in the world, for they are not of the world. Jesus paints a picture of the disciples versus the world: us versus them.

This theme is so common in our lives perhaps we don't even recognize how influential it is. Consider this: if I asked you what you think of Senate Democrats, what's the first emotion that comes to mind? Probably it's a strong emotion, whether positive or negative. Either you strongly feel that Senate Democrats are part of your "us" or part of your "them."

If I asked you how you feel about conservatives, what's the first emotion that comes to mind? Probably, again, a strong one. Either conservatives are a part of your "us," resulting in a strong positive emotion, or conservatives are part of your "them," eliciting a strong negative emotion.

In other words, if the word "Democrat" or "liberal" makes you recoil, feel revolted, or fearful because you believe they will ruin the country, that's a strong negative emotion. Liberals and Democrats are part of your "them," and thus you—and those like you (your "us")—are set against them.

I could name any number of other groups and many of us would have strong reactions one way or the other. This is how we see the world: us versus them; a tribal way of viewing things.

That's the word sociologists use to describe our divisive nature as a people: tribal. We might think of tribal politics, but it applies to any way in which we divide ourselves from others.

And certainly Jesus sounds like he's praying for his tribe. He knows he's on the way to the cross and that his time on earth is nearly done. He wants to make sure his disciples, and the disciples who will come after, all the way to us in this present day, are provided for, are cared for, are protected from "them," opposing tribes.

Jesus prays for his tribe, his us, the us of all disciples. We today would call that population Christians, a word Jesus didn't have in his vocabulary. But we might as well also call it a tribe. For that's what we are, that's how we identify. We're a tribe, and we're set against those who are set against us. We're set against those who would attack our beliefs, our way of life, our freedom to do and believe as we please.

We would attack.

It's an us-versus-them world out there. It's a dog-eat-dog world. It's an evil world full of malice. It's survival of the fittest. Darwin was right: Natural selection occurs, so we must make sure we're the strongest so we can stand up to whatever attacks come our way—so that when we attack back, we win.

This is where we are in our world at the moment. The lives which we live are full of division, both division we choose because we believe so much in our particular tribe, and division forced upon us. This, too, is where Christianity is at this moment. Our faith sees itself pitted against forces that are against it, putting us in a defensive posture. Division is so characteristic of our lives today we could say that division is the primary characteristic of the society in which we live and move and have our being.

How curious then that Jesus prays that his disciples become one.

His famous prayer for unity begins in John 17:20. After the talk of the world, after the request that the Father protect the disciples, Jesus prays that they may all be one, just as he and the Father are one. He prays for unity, and not just a nice, feel good, "I'd like to buy the world a soda" kind of unity. No, it's a unity about becoming one with the Father and each other, just as he and the Father are one.

This is radical unity. Consider the Trinity: We believe the Father, Son, and Holy Spirit are all one, yet simultaneously exist in distinct ways. We call this hypostatic union. That fancy theological term states what Jesus poignantly says: that he and the Father, along with the Holy Spirit, are all one. They are of the same stuff, the same mind—the mind he wants his disciples to have.

It's just like Paul says often throughout his letters and most famously in Philippians, "Let the same mind be in you that was in Christ Jesus" (Phil. 2:5). Stop and think of that for a second: the same mind as Christ. That would be the same mind as the Father, for the Father and Son are one. Jesus is praying that the disciples, both the eleven who remained and all those who would come after, including us, would have the same mind as the Father, would be one with the Father.

What are we to make of this kind of radical unity?

What are we to make of this kind of radical unity considering the divisive world in which we live?

Does Jesus want the disciples to have this radical unity with the Father so they can stand up against attacks and attack back those who would do harm to them? So that, when the world attacks, when "they" attack, disciples—Christians, we—can attack back and be successful? That's what us versus them would suggest.

Does Jesus want this radical unity so that the "us" will grow stronger against the "them" of the world?

Does Jesus pray for this radical unity so that, in the epic struggle of us versus them, we, us, will win?

At the end of this passage, Jesus says why he wants this unity, this oneness with the Father, for his disciples: so that the disciples may know the glory of God and may experience the love of God. And furthermore, that through the disciples, the world would know this same glory and love. His prayer is for glory and for love through the disciples for all the world.

The glory of God—like standing on a mountaintop looking at a vista, swept away by the glorious sight of creation. The glory of God—like holding a newborn baby. The glory of God—like witnessing acts of self-sacrifice, generosity, or even being the recipient of those. And this is but a taste of the glory of God—a glory that enlivens our souls. Jesus prays that the disciples would know the glory so their souls would be enlivened with the love of God.

The love of God. A love that is beyond what we can ask or imagine. But Paul gets us close: God's love is patient, kind, not envious or boastful or rude, but delighting in goodness, hopes in all circumstances, never ceases to believe, and in all these things, never fails (1 Cor. 13:4-8a). That's God, that's God's love, and that's what Jesus wants the disciples to know most of all because of their unity, their oneness with God: God's love.

Note that none of these things have anything to do with attacking, fighting, or winning. None of them speak to us versus them. In fact, here things are quite the opposite. So what are we to make of Jesus talking about "the world" and asking for protection for the disciples from the world and then asking for the disciples to have unity that leads to experiencing God's glory and love, things that seem antithetical to us versus them?

What, indeed, in our us versus them time, are we to make of this?

We need a mindset change.

When Jesus speaks of the world, even when Jesus speaks of being protected from the world, he's not speaking of "them." He's speaking of the way evil has separated and corrupted the world. Evil is a malevolent force in the world, and God is moving in power to undo it, but evil is not a them.

For with God, there is no them. There is merely a separation, a distance, between God and some of God's creation. And God mourns that separation. God laments that any of creation would be at a distance from God's love. Those who are at a distance are not a "them," for when God looks at humanity, when God looks at creation, God sees only us.

How? Because we, all of us, bear the image of God. When looking at creation, God sees creation as it was when God first created. Consider Genesis 1:31, "God saw everything that he had made, and indeed, it was very good" (NRSV). For God, it is still good. It is corrupted by the presence of evil in the world, but that doesn't mean that God rejects those parts that are corrupted.

For in order for God to view the world through an us-versus-them lens, that's what God would have to do: Reject part of his good creation. But God created all in his own image and cannot reject himself. So it is impossible for God to see the world in an us-versus-them lens. For God, no part of creation is irredeemable. For God, no one is beyond God's love, because God still loves his creation and calls it good.

And so there is no us versus them. It is antithetical to Christian theology. That's a fancy way of saying there's no way to be a disciple, a Christian, and see the world as us versus them. There is no way for us, as Christians, to hold that mentality. We are human, and it's in our nature to see the world through tribal lenses. But that's not something to accept; us versus them is an evil in our world to work against. It's a sin to rid ourselves of.

Throughout his letters, Paul says what Jesus asks for here: that there is now, because of Christ, no Jew nor Gentile, the primary us versus them of the New Testament. We can then say that, now, there is no Republican nor Democrat, no liberal nor conservative, no progressive nor traditionalist, no us versus them. There are simply humans, beloved of God.

And the way in which we learn to see the world through the eyes of God, to see the world through the love of God, to see the world without our tribal lenses that turn everyone we see into an us versus them, the way we learn to see the world through the eyes of God is through prayer.

Jesus, here, is praying. He's praying for unity, for oneness of mind, between the Father and his disciples. When Paul offers his words about there being now no us-versus-them any longer because of Christ, he's saying it as a prayer for the churches to whom he writes. We have in Jesus and Paul examples of how to rid ourselves of this evil, this sin, of an us versus them mentality: We pray.

Perhaps there is no better definition of prayer than this: to become of one mind with God. This is not to say that prayer makes us into God. Far from it, but prayer causes us to see the world the way God does. Prayer teaches us the character of God. Prayer transforms our minds and our hearts because prayer puts us in touch with God's glory and especially God's love, which is God's chief characteristic.

Praying the Psalms daily is perhaps the best way to get started with this life of prayer that makes us of one mind with the Father. It teaches us how to relate to God, gives our souls the language of prayer, and grounds our prayer life in scripture. To begin, read Psalm 1 today, and then keep going. (A suggested schedule is located in Appendix 4.)

Prayer makes us of one mind with the Father. It changes how we see the world. And that one mind, the more we gain it, cannot see the world in us-versus-them lenses. There are, instead, humans, all of us sinful and in need of mercy and grace.

Through the lens of prayer, as we become of one mind with the Father, we see our common humanity in everyone, everywhere. We see God when we look at each other because we all, even if we do not claim his name, bear the image of God. That was how we were created and that is how we remain. And because we all bear the image of God, we are all beloved of God, no matter how much of a "them" they may be in our minds.

Scripture says, "The prayers of a righteous person are powerful and effective" (James 5:16). They transform our vision, our lenses, to see the world as God does, rather than as our sinful, evil us-versus-them mentalities teach us to see the world. That's the power of prayer. That's why it's so important to pray. Commit yourself to the life of prayer.

If you're not sure where to begin, pray the Psalms daily, transforming your us versus them into seeing the world as God does: everyone bearing God's image, united as God's children. God is there in that moment of prayer, ready to meet you, changing your vision of the world.

When we meet God in prayer, we rise above tribalism. We move beyond the us-versus-them mentality. We get past biases, prejudices, and even hatred for those we once regarded as them. For there is no longer us versus them. There is only us, humans, children of God, images of God, beloved of God.

May we only see the world in just that way. Pray.

# Chapter 13

## PRAYER BRINGS US HOME

*Scripture Reading: Psalm 84*

Prayer should ultimately lead us ever deeper into the heart of God. That is where we are ultimately changed, transformed, and grown in Christlikeness to be a powerful force for good in the world. As we progress in our regular practice of prayer, we discover our true home.

Let us begin.

Each fall, I bet many of us schedule some pilgrimages. Each fall, we have a pilgrimage ritual, whether we realize it or not. We load up the car, go to great pains in preparation, making sure we have everything we need. That includes making sure we have the right gear for the big day when we have reached our pilgrimage site. These pilgrimages we'll make require advanced preparation, even some headaches in taking time out of our normal lives. But I bet we all agree, it's worth it.

I make pilgrimages myself most falls. Last fall, I had one planned but then Dana came down with pneumonia, so our pilgrimage was cancelled. Back then, and even this fall, in my mind's eye I see myself preparing for a pilgrimage like we all make: booking a hotel room, ordering my family the right gear for the big day, taking a day off work, maybe even missing a Sunday in worship, just to make this pilgrimage. We'd hit the road on a Thursday or Friday with an aim to be in Harrisonburg, Virginia, our pilgrimage site, on Saturday, for that's the big day!

On that pilgrimage Saturday, we'd don our James Madison University football gear. I can see Jackson and Carter in their JMU T-shirts, both of them standing with the giant Duke Dog mascot statue in front of the football stadium. Then we'd go in and cheer on the Dukes to victory!

Beforehand, of course, there would be some rituals to teach; some football habits.

That would include standard cheers but, of course, they already know the fight song. Then we'd go to the game, cheer our hearts out, and take the time to move around the campus, reminiscing and telling stories.

This is the pilgrimage many of us make during the fall: to a football game, but to so much more than that. We go back to our former homes, places that even still feel like home, back to where we left a part of our hearts, back to a symbol that carries great meaning. We take time, we go to the expense, we invite friends, we gather with family, not just to cheer on our team, but to recover a sense of self, a part of us that gets lost in the day-to-day shuffle.

The pilgrimage I have described to JMU, while difficult in some ways, tiring in its length and energy expended, would be worth it. It'd be worth it to be able to go back to campus, back to the feelings evoked by my alma mater, back to my home.

I bet many of you would agree when thinking of your alma mater or your favorite team.

Whenever one of my alma maters comes up in conversation, my heart swells a little. The mere mention of their name brings forth memories of old, deep feelings of peace and joy and hope for the future. We long to rekindle those feelings and instill them in our loved ones. And thus, we make pilgrimages.

This fall, you'll want to make a pilgrimage to your alma mater. Maybe multiple pilgrimages. All for the sake of going home, going to where you feel like you belong, where you gain right perspective on life, where you find purpose and meaning warmed up nicely in the bread of nostalgia. You'll make the sacrifices of time, energy, and money to take this pilgrimage home.

Home, they say, is where the heart is. Many of us left parts of our hearts on college campuses. I spent nineteen years at Berry College, growing up there and then attending college there. Dana also attended there. A big part of our heart is on that campus.

In the spaces of college campuses, among the oak trees, the inspiring architecture, and the perfectly manicured grounds, we are reminded of who we are, of what life means to us, of our dreams, of our aspirations. We find the strength to continue to move to achieve those dreams or the strength to respond to the conviction that we have strayed off course.

Such is part of why I keep a picture on my computer desktop, a photo of the Candler School of Theology and Cannon Chapel at Emory University, two places near and dear to my heart. The photo has a way of calling my heart back to center, back to the faith that grew because of the formation I received in my years there.

Home, as a feeling as well as a place, has huge importance to us. So much so, that we're willing to make sacrifices to pilgrimage back.

Going home is what the scripture reading for this chapter is about. In reading t, it seems like it's talking about heaven: about literally standing in God's presence through God's courts. "How lovely is your dwelling place," the psalmist says. "I long to be there" he continues, asking to come into the courts of God. For there is true rest, true peace, true belonging, true sense of meaning and purpose in life, true refuge. For there, the psalmist says, is home. This sounds just like home as we desire it. And perhaps as we experience it when we make our pilgrimages.

Turns out, we're not the only ones who feel that way about Psalm 84. Johannes Brahms wrote *Ein deutsches Requiem (A German Requiem)* based on this psalm. It has been performed at funeral services often, echoing the sentiment that now the dead have realized what this psalmist knew in his mind's eye: the refuge, peace, joy, and complete fulfillment of making that final pilgrimage to God's presence, our true home.

For that is where we long to be in this life. Even if we don't realize it, we're built for union with God, for only in union with God can we truly find what we get for a moment on our college campuses and what this psalmist knows: the sense of meaning and purpose, the clarity of vision about the world and our place in it, the peace and rest from the trials of life, the refuge that comes when we go home.

It's tempting to read this psalm as only about our longing for our heavenly home. Our souls long, even faint, for that moment of true reunion with our creator. At moments, perhaps when we feel most foreign, most exposed, most vulnerable, most like we're not at home, we know we're missing our heavenly home. In such moments, perhaps you long to make a pilgrimage to some place that feels like home, maybe a college campus, maybe elsewhere. I know, when I am feeling most away from home in my heart, I long to make a pilgrimage to Berry, JMU, or Emory.

We long for home the way I can imagine the soldiers who first heard Bing Crosby's "I'll Be Home for Christmas" longed for home.

Crosby released the song in time for Christmas 1943, at the height of World War II, promising to be home for Christmas, if only in his heart. There, on the battlefields of Europe and the Pacific, soldiers could take themselves back to the nostalgia of a Christmas spent at home, with presents beneath the tree. They could make a mental and spiritual pilgrimage back to their homes, back to where they truly belonged, not this foreign, exposed, vulnerable moment of war, but back to where life makes sense, where belonging can be found, back to peace and joy and refuge.

We long for that kind of home because we're built for it. We long for it the way the pilgrims did in this psalm. For as much as we may think of the psalm as speaking of heaven in our modern era, the psalmist wrote it thinking about traveling to Jerusalem, to visit the temple, to go to the physical courtyard and visit God's literal dwelling place. The psalmist wanted to make the kind of pilgrimage we make to college campuses.

The psalmist wanted to go home.

For the ancients, this could literally be done. They believed God actually dwelled in the temple, and they could go visit, not in their dreams, but in reality.

But such a trip required sacrifice, not unlike when we make trips to our alma maters. The ancients had to interrupt their usual schedule, prepare ahead of time for the trip, teach their children the rituals and rules of the temple life, expend the time, energy, and money in travel, all to go and visit their home: Solomon's Temple in Jerusalem. It required preparation and sacrifice, but as the psalmist tells us, it's worth it, for better is one single day spent at the temple than a thousand days spent elsewhere.

We, too, can make that pilgrimage. Sure, those of us with the time and money can make the pilgrimage to the Temple Mount and see where the temple used to stand. We can pray at the Wailing Wall, which was part of this same temple.

But we are the people of Jesus. While the ancients believed that God literally dwelled in the temple, at Jesus's crucifixion the curtain separating God from the priests in that temple was torn. God resides in our hearts now, not in some physical locale. Jesus paved the way for us to make a spiritual pilgrimage to our home not over land, but in our hearts. We can go home any time we pause our lives, make the sacrifice, to pray and be present with God. Ours is a spiritual pilgrimage, a way of coming home in our hearts.

It's said that home is where the heart is. Which begs the question: Where's your heart?

Is your heart in the things of God? To come home to God in your heart requires first that God is in your heart. Have you committed your life to Christ?

If you have, then traveling home, at its simplest, is a matter of simply choosing to be with God through prayer as discussed throughout the book. That can be for a moment of prayer or meditation, or even just to pause and clear our minds before reading scripture or a devotional book. Regardless of the form, our pilgrimage come when we choose to pause our lives and travel home in our hearts.

But sometimes we need more than that. Sometimes we need the overland route, too, to make our pilgrimage back home. Sometimes we need to retreat away from the hustle and bustle of our everyday lives, from the familiar surroundings of our homes, in order to return to our spiritual homes.

That's the power college campuses can hold for many of us. In fact, sometimes pilgrimages to football games do just this for us: They hit the reset button by making us forget our everyday lives for a while to focus on family, fun, and fellowship. God is present in those moments with us.

But we have other places in our lives, too. Maybe you have a farm you retreat to. Maybe you go down to the river. Maybe you take a walk through your neighborhood. Maybe you go home to your parents or your children's house or a family piece of property.

Perhaps church is home. I know our church buildings have that feeling of home for many. Your church is a great place to make a pilgrimage, to come and worship, reflect, pray, journal, or simply sit in silence, doing whatever form of prayer works for you or trying out one of the forms in the appendices.

Home is where the heart is. Where is your heart?

Purposefully travel home in your heart. Go to that place, physical or in your soul, where life makes sense and you feel refreshed. It's not escapism, and it's not wimping out—it's self-care. The Gospels are full of accounts of Jesus going off by himself to be at home with his Father in his heart. Sometimes the world is too much. We preserve our witness to the world, we encourage our hearts to be good neighbors, by taking care of ourselves. Pilgrimages do that. If Jesus set that example of pilgrimage, we should do likewise.

Traveling home, going to God's presence, simply requires that we pause the rest of our lives. We pause when we take time at home to be with God in whatever form that takes. We pause when we take time to go to church, to dwell with God in prayer, or to go to special places in our lives where our hearts sense that feeling of home.

Rest and peace, refuge and strength, are ours when we travel to our spiritual home. There may be sacrifice involved, especially a sacrifice of time. But it's worth the sacrifice of time. As the choir in Brahms's Requiem sings:

Lord, let me know my end,
and what is the measure of my days;
let me know how fleeting my life is.
You have made my days a few handbreadths,
and my lifetime is as nothing in your sight.
Surely everyone stands as a mere breath.
Surely everyone goes about like a shadow.
Surely for nothing they are in turmoil;
they heap up, and do not know who will gather.
And now, O Lord, what do I wait for? My hope is in you.

How often is your life like this Psalm? "Surely for nothing [we] are in turmoil." We heap up, meaning we keep working, sometimes not even knowing why anymore. When that happens, when our hearts are in turmoil and we have lost our way, we find our way again when we return home; when we make a pilgrimage back to where life makes sense, back to where God seems more accessible, back to where we feel warm and accepted, back to our homes.

That's the power of regular, authentic, unceasing prayer. We become ever more acquainted with the pilgrimage route to our true home with God. There, we are changed, evermore characterized by the fruits of the Spirit, a people who can pray the profound yet of faith, ceding outcomes, and seeing the world as one beloved creation of God. This is the power of prayer to change us.

Go home. Make a pilgrimage through prayer to center your heart in God daily. Home is where the heart is.

Where is your heart?

# Conclusion

## ESTABLISHING A LIFE OF PRAYER

During a dark and difficult chapter in my own life, I discovered the power of prayer bringing me home. The position I held at that time required a forty-five-minute commute each way. As my work grew more difficult, as I felt increasingly assailed from all sides, I would turn on Taizé music and worship with it as I drove home. This became the form of prayer that worked for me in that moment, causing me to follow the well-worn pathway of prayer that leads straight to my home, at the heart of Christ.

As I prayed with this routine, I found the strength to do what was right, which was often counter to what I wanted to do. I found my vision of the world around me was renewed, such that I could empathize with the plight of those who were causing me harm, seeing their suffering, acknowledging that they were just as much a child of God as me. To be sure, there were times I did not feel so generous. In those moments, the pathway of prayer was littered with my complaints, objections, and condemnations. My prayer journal from that time records much authenticity, enough to make me blush today.

But this is how we are to pray: with authenticity, with forthrightness, with an openness in our hearts for us to be changed by our encounters with God. When we are brave enough to pray in this way, and when we do so with routine, we discover that we are changed, and for the better.

Prayer does, indeed, bring us home in our hearts. Our true homes are with Christ, and prayer—regular, authentic prayer as we have discussed in this book—paves the pathway to that true home.

This is the truth I have found in my own journey with prayer. The more I pray, the more often I find my way home. There, at home with Christ, I am changed. I grow in holiness, I learn to be more authentic as I grow in self-awareness, and I find the faith to deal with the challenges and difficulties of life. This is how we are changed by prayer: We grow in faith, we grow in holiness, and we grow in Christlikeness.

The world needs more people who are Christlike, or what Methodists would say are more people following the path of sanctification. That is our fancy way of talking about growing in love, being shaped and molded by our experiences with Christ, such that we are able to live out who Christ is to the world—the best of us.

Perhaps, here at the end, that is the best way to describe how prayer changes us: It makes us the best of who God designed us to be. The Enneagram talks about how the pursuit of self-awareness unlocks the "true self," which is the gift of who God designed us to be, meant to be shared with the world. As we walk the pathway of prayer, doing so on a regular basis with authenticity, we grow in self-awareness, bringing our sins and wounds before God for healing, finding ourselves transformed by our encounters into a people who see the world as God sees the world. Then, as we are shaped and molded, more and more of our true self comes out. We become increasingly a gift to the world.

Prayer changes us. As you have read, I hope you have discovered the power of prayer to change you. The following pages of appendixes are designed to help you cultivate a habit of prayer, a routine, using a type of prayer that works for you. Experiment with them; see which ones cause you to feel the most connected to God. Just as we all have a true self that's a gift to the world, we are all designed differently by our creator, and thus a form of prayer that works well for one person may not work as well for you. That is OK, for the key here is to experiment and find a means of creating a habit of prayer that will last.

To establish such a habit, pray at the same time every day. Link your act of prayer to something you already do. If you do this daily for a month, you will naturally yearn for that habit of prayer whenever you engage in that thing you already do. For example, when I learned this trick, I began to pray immediately after I poured my second cup of coffee in the morning. Now when I pour that second cup, I naturally yearn to pray. In this way, the habit becomes routine; I hardly have to remind myself to engage in prayer.[1]

Wherever you are, and however routine your prayer life may be currently, take the time to engage in prayer daily. Find a way of praying that works for you. Establish it as a habit, a routine, such that you walk the pathway of prayer daily. That journey will no doubt transform you, change you, grow you in Christlikeness. That's the power of prayer to change us.

St. Benedict of Nursia is famous for saying, "Always, we begin again." Throughout

---

1. For more reading on this, check out Charles Duhigg's great book on habits titled *The Power of Habit*.

this book, I have used the phrase, "Let us begin." The practice of prayer requires a willingness to begin again. No matter how disciplined and routine we become in our habits, they will from time to time falter and fail. We will sin and need to repent before we can easily find our way back to the pathway of prayer. The darkness will sometimes be so overwhelming that no amount of habit and practice could allow us to find the way back until the light of Christ shows us the way. To engage in the practice of prayer is always to be willing to begin again.

Mindful of this, and all that has come before in this book, I say to myself as well as to you, the reader:

Let us begin.

# Appendix 1

## DIFFERENT TYPES OF PRAYER AND RESOURCE GUIDE

### Praying Scripture (Lectio Divina)

Here is a guide to praying scripture called Lectio Divina. It may be used with any scripture, so feel free to pick some of your favorites or simply turn to any random page. For a suggested list of scriptures per day see Appendix 5.

*The Process: Four Stages to Praying Scripture*

| Stage | Question | Task |
|---|---|---|
| Phrase | What phrase stands out to you? | Listen for the answer |
| Word | What word stands out to you? | Listen for the answer |
| Message | What is God telling you? | Listen for the answer |
| Prayer | Tell God what you heard | Listen for the answer |

*The Flow for Each Stage:*

What to do in each stage of the process

| Movement | Task |
|---|---|
| Silence | Be still and quiet and in a mindset of prayer. |
| Reading | Listen for an answer to the question for the stage. |
| Silence | Be present with the answer you hear. |
| Sharing | Share with God what you're hearing. |

### Intercessory Prayer

There are many models for this. In its simplest form, intercessory prayer is telling God about the needs in your life and the concerns that weigh on your heart, whether for you and those you love or those things in your community and around the world that are cause for concern.

One of my favorite models is ACTS:

Adoration: Tell God how awesome God is and what you love about God.

Contrition: Tell God of your sins, confessing where you need God's mercy and grace.

Thanksgiving: Tell God thank you for forgiving your sins and for anything else in your life for which you are grateful.

Supplication: Tell God what you need and the needs of others.

**Prayer Journaling**

Keeping a prayer journal is a great way to pray. It can be a space for intercessory prayer, bringing our needs before God. It is also a powerful tool in becoming more self-aware. In the pages we keep, we are able to work out our challenges, discover new things about ourselves, and find our path forward. This is especially helpful for anyone who thinks best by writing, drawing, or creating flow charts.

To begin a prayer journal, find a notebook or an app that you will use only for this purpose. That singularity of use is key because it teaches our brains to focus on self-reflection and prayer whenever we sit down with that notebook or app.

If you write, free write, just like in school. Just tell God whatever is on your heart and just begin. This is very informal and, in fact, any attempt at formality through proper grammar or formatting will get in the way of doing the work the prayer journal is designed to do.

If you are predisposed to drawing or flow-charts, draw those instead of writing. Color in the pages if that's helpful to you. Do whatever will help you express yourself before God, bringing all of your sense of self before God, allowing space to be changed.

Keep it private. This is where you are pouring out your heart to God. It should be for your eyes only.

From time to time, look back at previous entries to see how God has provided for you in the past.

**Contemplative Prayer**

Contemplative prayer is a way of praying that rarely involves us speaking. It's markedly different from any of the ways discussed earlier in this appendix. That's because we seek to silence ourselves and our minds to simply be in God's presence, only aware of either our breath or whatever it is we happen to be giving our focus to (e.g., contemplating). Here are different methods:

Sitting in silence: Exactly what it sounds like as we clear our minds to be only with God's presence. Sometimes this is referred to as meditation or Christian meditation.

Singing along with worship music: If we can simply focus our energies with our favorite worship music, this is a form of contemplative prayer

Repetition: As discussed in chapter 4, praying the same phrase or word over and over again, simply sitting with those words to give God space to speak truth into our lives.

Lectio Divina: This way of praying with scripture mentioned earlier is a form of contemplative prayer.

Pray without ceasing: As discussed in chapter 7, praying while engaging in anything we do that connects us to God's presence and to our true self simply means to make ourselves available to God and aware of God's presence. This could happen through gardening, cleaning, or any other of a number of activities.

## Make a Pilgrimage

As discussed in chapter 13, pilgrimages are great ways to get back in touch with our true selves when life has distracted us away. To make such a pilgrimage prayerful, plan to go to a place where your heart feels at home and at peace. While there, steal away to a favorite spot by yourself to engage in a method of praying, whether that's bringing your journal, praying with scripture, meditating, or doing some other form of prayer. Plan to spend this part of the pilgrimage in solitude, a great way to get back in touch with your true self and with God by being apart from others. Then, when you have finished, tell someone about your experience. Celebrate together how you have found God.

## Prayer Guides

Using a daily prayer guide is a great way to establish a daily habit. Three options that church members and my family have found useful are *The Divine Hours* by Phyllis Tickle, *A Guide to Prayer for All God's People* by Reuben P. Job and Norman Shawchuck, and *Common Prayer* by Shane Claiborne, Jonathan Wilson, and Enuma Okoro. Of course, there are many other options as well.

Also helpful are seasonal devotionals or prayer guides, usually focused on the seasons of Advent and Lent. These will often feature small prayers and spaces for reflection. There are a ton of options available at your favorite retailer for these seasons and others. I have often found adding one of these to my usual routine helps me stay focused on the seasons of Advent and Lent.

# Appendix 2

## ELEMENTS OF PRAYER FROM THE LORD'S PRAYER

This is a particular method of prayer taught by the Lord's Prayer, as highlighted in chapter 4. It can be a model for personal prayer or a way of understanding the power of repeating the Lord's Prayer itself as a part of our daily practice.

Address to God (our Father)

Praise of God (hallowed be your name)

Submission to God's will (your kingdom come, your will be done, on earth as it is in heaven)

Petition for needs to be met (give us this day our daily bread)

Statement of humility (forgive us our trespasses)

Recognition of our humanity (as we forgive those who trespass against us)

Request for help (Lead us not into temptation, but deliver us from evil).

Try praying these seven items in your prayer journal.

# Appendix 3

## JOHN WESLEY'S SELF-EXAMINATION
## QUESTIONS FOR HOLY CLUBS

These are the questions referenced in chapter 9 that help create self-awareness. As Wesley did in his holy clubs, consider asking yourself these questions once a week and then praying the responses back to God, discovering where you're in need of God's mercy and grace to offer forgiveness and healing.

Am I consciously or unconsciously creating the impression that I am better than I really am?

Am I honest in all my acts and words, or do I exaggerate?

Do I confidentially pass on to another what was told to me in confidence?

Can I be trusted?

Am I a slave to dress, friends, work, or habits?

Am I self-conscious, self-pitying, or self-justifying?

Did the Bible live in me today?

Do I give it time to speak to me every day?

Am I enjoying praying?

When did I last speak to someone else of my faith?

Do I pray about the money I spend?

Do I get to bed on time and get up on time?

Do I disobey God in anything?

Do I insist upon doing something about why my conscience is uneasy?

Am I defeated in any part of my life?

Am I jealous, impure, critical, irritable, touchy, or distrustful?

How do I spend my spare time?

Am I proud?

Do I thank God that I am not as other people, especially the Pharisees who despised the publican?

Is there anyone whom I fear, dislike, disown, criticize, hold a resentment toward or disregard? If so, what am I doing about it?

Do I grumble or complain constantly?

Is Christ real to me?

# Appendix 4

## PRAYING THE PSALMS SCHEDULE

Referenced in several chapters, this is the schedule for praying the Psalms. The schedule begins with Day One, rather than a date, so that your practice can begin on any day of the year. The schedule proceeds by repeating the same reading twice, allowing our souls time to absorb what we find there.

Some psalms are divided up into smaller segments, better allowing us to hear God speak. Consider praying these psalms using the method described in Appendix 1 under "Praying Scripture."

| Day | Psalm |
| --- | --- |
| 1 | Psalm 1 |
| 2 | Psalm 1 |
| 3 | Psalm 2 |
| 4 | Psalm 2 |
| 5 | Psalm 3 |
| 6 | Psalm 3 |
| 7 | Psalm 4 |
| 8 | Psalm 4 |
| 9 | Psalm 5 |
| 10 | Psalm 5 |
| 11 | Psalm 6 |
| 12 | Psalm 6 |
| 13 | Psalm 7 |
| 14 | Psalm 7 |
| 15 | Psalm 8 |
| 16 | Psalm 8 |
| 17 | Psalm 9:1-10 |
| 18 | Psalm 9:1-10 |
| 19 | Psalm 9:11-20 |
| 20 | Psalm 9:11-20 |
| 21 | Psalm 10 |
| 22 | Psalm 10 |
| 23 | Psalm 11 |

118

| | |
|---|---|
| 24 | Psalm 11 |
| 25 | Psalm 12 |
| 26 | Psalm 12 |
| 27 | Psalm 13 |
| 28 | Psalm 13 |
| 29 | Psalm 14 |
| 30 | Psalm 14 |
| 31 | Psalm 15 |
| 32 | Psalm 15 |
| 33 | Psalm 16 |
| 34 | Psalm 16 |
| 35 | Psalm 17 |
| 36 | Psalm 17 |
| 37 | Psalm 18:1-24 |
| 38 | Psalm 18:1-24 |
| 39 | Psalm 18:25-50 |
| 40 | Psalm 18:25-50 |
| 41 | Psalm 19 |
| 42 | Psalm 19 |
| 43 | Psalm 20 |
| 44 | Psalm 20 |
| 45 | Psalm 21 |
| 46 | Psalm 21 |
| 47 | Psalm 22:1-21 |
| 48 | Psalm 22:1-21 |
| 49 | Psalm 22:22-31 |
| 50 | Psalm 22:22-31 |
| 51 | Psalm 23 |
| 52 | Psalm 23 |
| 53 | Psalm 24 |
| 54 | Psalm 24 |
| 55 | Psalm 25 |
| 56 | Psalm 25 |
| 57 | Psalm 26 |
| 58 | Psalm 26 |

| | |
|---|---|
| 59 | Psalm 27 |
| 60 | Psalm 27 |
| 61 | Psalm 28 |
| 62 | Psalm 28 |
| 63 | Psalm 29 |
| 64 | Psalm 29 |
| 65 | Psalm 30 |
| 66 | Psalm 30 |
| 67 | Psalm 31 |
| 68 | Psalm 31 |
| 69 | Psalm 32 |
| 70 | Psalm 32 |
| 71 | Psalm 33 |
| 72 | Psalm 33 |
| 73 | Psalm 34 |
| 74 | Psalm 34 |
| 75 | Psalm 35:1-16 |
| 76 | Psalm 35:1-16 |
| 77 | Psalm 35:17-28 |
| 78 | Psalm 35:17-28 |
| 79 | Psalm 36 |
| 80 | Psalm 36 |
| 81 | Psalm 37:1-20 |
| 82 | Psalm 37:1-20 |
| 83 | Psalm 37:21-40 |
| 84 | Psalm 37:21-40 |
| 85 | Psalm 38:1-11 |
| 86 | Psalm 38:1-11 |
| 87 | Psalm 38:12-22 |
| 88 | Psalm 38:12-22 |
| 89 | Psalm 39 |
| 90 | Psalm 39 |
| 91 | Psalm 40 |
| 92 | Psalm 40 |
| 93 | Psalm 41 |

| 94 | Psalm 41 |
|---|---|
| 95 | Psalm 42 |
| 96 | Psalm 42 |
| 97 | Psalm 43 |
| 98 | Psalm 43 |
| 99 | Psalm 44:1-16 |
| 100 | Psalm 44:1-16 |
| 101 | Psalm 44:17-26 |
| 102 | Psalm 44:17-26 |
| 103 | Psalm 45 |
| 104 | Psalm 45 |
| 105 | Psalm 46 |
| 106 | Psalm 46 |
| 107 | Psalm 47 |
| 108 | Psalm 47 |
| 109 | Psalm 48 |
| 110 | Psalm 48 |
| 111 | Psalm 49 |
| 112 | Psalm 49 |
| 113 | Psalm 50:1-15 |
| 114 | Psalm 50:1-15 |
| 115 | Psalm 50:16-23 |
| 116 | Psalm 50:16-23 |
| 117 | Psalm 51 |
| 118 | Psalm 51 |
| 119 | Psalm 52 |
| 120 | Psalm 52 |
| 121 | Psalm 53 |
| 122 | Psalm 53 |
| 123 | Psalm 54 |
| 124 | Psalm 54 |
| 125 | Psalm 55 |
| 126 | Psalm 55 |
| 127 | Psalm 56 |
| 128 | Psalm 56 |

| 129 | Psalm 57 |
| 130 | Psalm 57 |
| 131 | Psalm 58 |
| 132 | Psalm 58 |
| 133 | Psalm 59 |
| 134 | Psalm 59 |
| 135 | Psalm 60 |
| 136 | Psalm 60 |
| 137 | Psalm 61 |
| 138 | Psalm 61 |
| 139 | Psalm 62 |
| 140 | Psalm 62 |
| 141 | Psalm 63 |
| 142 | Psalm 63 |
| 143 | Psalm 64 |
| 144 | Psalm 64 |
| 145 | Psalm 65 |
| 146 | Psalm 65 |
| 147 | Psalm 66 |
| 148 | Psalm 66 |
| 149 | Psalm 67 |
| 150 | Psalm 67 |
| 151 | Psalm 68:1-16 |
| 152 | Psalm 68:1-16 |
| 153 | Psalm 68:17-35 |
| 154 | Psalm 68:17-36 |
| 155 | Psalm 69:1-15 |
| 156 | Psalm 69:1-15 |
| 157 | Psalm 69:16-36 |
| 158 | Psalm 69:16-36 |
| 159 | Psalm 70 |
| 160 | Psalm 70 |
| 161 | Psalm 71 |
| 162 | Psalm 71 |
| 163 | Psalm 72 |

| 164 | Psalm 72 |
| --- | --- |
| 165 | Psalm 73:1-14 |
| 166 | Psalm 73:1-14 |
| 167 | Psalm 73:15-28 |
| 168 | Psalm 73:15-28 |
| 169 | Psalm 74 |
| 170 | Psalm 74 |
| 171 | Psalm 75 |
| 172 | Psalm 75 |
| 173 | Psalm 76 |
| 174 | Psalm 76 |
| 175 | Psalm 77 |
| 176 | Psalm 77 |
| 177 | Psalm 78:1-16 |
| 178 | Psalm 78:1-16 |
| 179 | Psalm 78:17-55 |
| 180 | Psalm 78:17-55 |
| 181 | Psalm 78:56-72 |
| 182 | Psalm 78:56-72 |
| 183 | Psalm 79 |
| 184 | Psalm 79 |
| 185 | Psalm 80 |
| 186 | Psalm 80 |
| 187 | Psalm 81 |
| 188 | Psalm 81 |
| 189 | Psalm 82 |
| 190 | Psalm 82 |
| 191 | Psalm 83 |
| 192 | Psalm 83 |
| 193 | Psalm 84 |
| 194 | Psalm 84 |
| 195 | Psalm 85 |
| 196 | Psalm 85 |
| 197 | Psalm 86 |
| 198 | Psalm 86 |

| 199 | Psalm 87 |
| 200 | Psalm 87 |
| 201 | Psalm 88 |
| 202 | Psalm 88 |
| 203 | Psalm 89:1-18 |
| 204 | Psalm 89:1-18 |
| 205 | Psalm 89:13-37 |
| 206 | Psalm 89:13-37 |
| 207 | Psalm 89:38-52 |
| 208 | Psalm 89:38-52 |
| 209 | Psalm 90 |
| 210 | Psalm 90 |
| 211 | Psalm 91 |
| 212 | Psalm 91 |
| 213 | Psalm 92 |
| 214 | Psalm 92 |
| 215 | Psalm 93 |
| 216 | Psalm 93 |
| 217 | Psalm 94 |
| 218 | Psalm 94 |
| 219 | Psalm 95 |
| 220 | Psalm 95 |
| 221 | Psalm 96 |
| 222 | Psalm 96 |
| 223 | Psalm 97 |
| 224 | Psalm 97 |
| 225 | Psalm 98 |
| 226 | Psalm 98 |
| 227 | Psalm 99 |
| 228 | Psalm 99 |
| 229 | Psalm 100 |
| 230 | Psalm 100 |
| 231 | Psalm 101 |
| 232 | Psalm 101 |
| 233 | Psalm 102:1-17 |

| | |
|---|---|
| 234 | Psalm 102:1-17 |
| 235 | Psalm 102:18-28 |
| 236 | Psalm 102:18-28 |
| 237 | Psalm 103 |
| 238 | Psalm 103 |
| 239 | Psalm 104:1-23 |
| 240 | Psalm 104:1-23 |
| 241 | Psalm 104:24-35 |
| 242 | Psalm 104:24-35 |
| 243 | Psalm 105:1-25 |
| 244 | Psalm 105:1-25 |
| 245 | Psalm 105:26-45 |
| 246 | Psalm 105:26-45 |
| 247 | Psalm 106:1-23 |
| 248 | Psalm 106:1-23 |
| 249 | Psalm 106:24-39 |
| 250 | Psalm 106:24-39 |
| 251 | Psalm 106:40-48 |
| 252 | Psalm 106:40-48 |
| 253 | Psalm 107:1-22 |
| 254 | Psalm 107:1-22 |
| 255 | Psalm 107:23-43 |
| 256 | Psalm 107:23-43 |
| 257 | Psalm 108 |
| 258 | Psalm 108 |
| 259 | Psalm 109 |
| 260 | Psalm 109 |
| 261 | Psalm 110 |
| 262 | Psalm 110 |
| 263 | Psalm 111 |
| 264 | Psalm 111 |
| 265 | Psalm 112 |
| 266 | Psalm 112 |
| 267 | Psalm 113 |
| 268 | Psalm 113 |

| | |
|---|---|
| 269 | Psalm 114 |
| 270 | Psalm 114 |
| 271 | Psalm 115 |
| 272 | Psalm 115 |
| 273 | Psalm 116 |
| 274 | Psalm 116 |
| 275 | Psalm 117 |
| 276 | Psalm 117 |
| 277 | Psalm 118 |
| 278 | Psalm 118 |
| 279 | Psalm 119:1-16 |
| 280 | Psalm 119:1-16 |
| 281 | Psalm 119:17-32 |
| 282 | Psalm 119:17-32 |
| 283 | Psalm 119:33-48 |
| 284 | Psalm 119:33-48 |
| 285 | Psalm 119:49-64 |
| 286 | Psalm 119:49-64 |
| 287 | Psalm 119:65-80 |
| 288 | Psalm 119:65-80 |
| 289 | Psalm 119:81-96 |
| 290 | Psalm 119:81-96 |
| 291 | Psalm 119:97-112 |
| 292 | Psalm 119:97-112 |
| 293 | Psalm 119:113-128 |
| 294 | Psalm 119:113-128 |
| 295 | Psalm 119:129-144 |
| 296 | Psalm 119:129-144 |
| 297 | Psalm 119:145-160 |
| 298 | Psalm 119:145-160 |
| 299 | Psalm 119:161-176 |
| 300 | Psalm 119:161-176 |
| 301 | Psalm 120 |
| 302 | Psalm 120 |
| 303 | Psalm 121 |

| | |
|---|---|
| 304 | Psalm 121 |
| 305 | Psalm 122 |
| 306 | Psalm 122 |
| 307 | Psalm 123 |
| 308 | Psalm 123 |
| 309 | Psalm 124 |
| 310 | Psalm 124 |
| 311 | Psalm 125 |
| 312 | Psalm 125 |
| 313 | Psalm 126 |
| 314 | Psalm 126 |
| 315 | Psalm 127 |
| 316 | Psalm 127 |
| 317 | Psalm 128 |
| 318 | Psalm 128 |
| 319 | Psalm 129 |
| 320 | Psalm 129 |
| 321 | Psalm 130 |
| 322 | Psalm 130 |
| 323 | Psalm 131 |
| 324 | Psalm 131 |
| 325 | Psalm 132 |
| 326 | Psalm 132 |
| 327 | Psalm 133 |
| 328 | Psalm 133 |
| 329 | Psalm 134 |
| 330 | Psalm 134 |
| 331 | Psalm 135 |
| 332 | Psalm 135 |
| 333 | Psalm 136:1-9 |
| 334 | Psalm 136:1-9 |
| 335 | Psalm 136:10-26 |
| 336 | Psalm 136:10-26 |
| 337 | Psalm 137 |
| 338 | Psalm 137 |

| 339 | Psalm 138 |
| 340 | Psalm 138 |
| 341 | Psalm 139 |
| 342 | Psalm 139 |
| 343 | Psalm 140 |
| 344 | Psalm 140 |
| 345 | Psalm 141 |
| 346 | Psalm 141 |
| 347 | Psalm 142 |
| 348 | Psalm 142 |
| 349 | Psalm 143 |
| 350 | Psalm 143 |
| 351 | Psalm 144 |
| 352 | Psalm 144 |
| 353 | Psalm 145 |
| 354 | Psalm 145 |
| 355 | Psalm 146 |
| 356 | Psalm 146 |
| 357 | Psalm 147 |
| 358 | Psalm 147 |
| 359 | Psalm 148 |
| 360 | Psalm 148 |
| 361 | Psalm 149 |
| 362 | Psalm 149 |
| 363 | Psalm 150 |
| 364 | Psalm 150 |

# Appendix 5

## DAILY BIBLE READING SCHEDULE

Below is a schedule for reading the Bible in a year as an act of prayer. It can be used with Lectio Divina (see Appendix 1). The schedule offers four different categories. Those wishing to create a daily practice of reading the Bible might start with reading just one of the categories. Changing categories yearly would result in reading the whole Bible in four years. Or, categories may be combined two or three at a time. The most ambitious will read all four daily.

A note on each of the tracks:

### General Note

The Old Testament is divided into three sections: History, Teachings, and Prophets. All three trace the same history in chronological order: creation of the Israelites as a people, journey to the land, living in the land of Canaan, establishment of the Kingdom of Israel, the destruction and exile of the same, and the return from exile. Each, however, traces that history differently. As such, some tracks contain readings from other tracks.

### History

We trace the story through the stories the Israelites told, from the very beginnings of the universe through the return from exile. You'll note that this track contains the Torah, the first five books, but eliminates the portions that are law. Those are contained within the wisdom track.

### Teachings

In teachings, the story picks up with what is probably the oldest part of the Old Testament: Job. It then moves into wisdom and the law. The law was given while the Israelites journeyed to the land. Interspersed are psalms, again in chronological order. For those praying the psalms daily, note that this schedule is very different from that one.

### Prophets

We pick up the story near the end of the Kingdom of Israel. All the prophets in the Old Testament prophesied during the end of the kingdom, the exile, and the first years of the return from exile. Interspersed among the prophets are references to history books like 2 Kings or Ezra. This is to give the historical context for the work of the prophet.

**New Testament**

Finally, the New Testament track goes back and forth between Gospels and letters. When reading, it becomes easy to get bogged down in one style of writing, so instead this schedule keeps us engaged through variety. It opens with the New Testament's best introduction of who Jesus is and what Jesus means in the context of the history of the Old Testament and then moves forward through the life and teachings of Jesus.

| Day | History | Teachings | Prophets | New Testament |
|---|---|---|---|---|
| Day 1 | Genesis 1:1-2:4a | Job 1 | 2 Kings 14:23-29 | Hebrews 1 |
| Day 2 | Genesis 2:4b-24 | Job 2 | 2 Kings 15:1-7 | Hebrews 2 |
| Day 3 | Genesis 3 | Job 3 | 2 Chronicles 26:1-15 | Hebrews 3 |
| Day 4 | Genesis 4 | Job 4 | 2 Chronicles 26:16-22 | Hebrews 4 |
| Day 5 | Genesis 5 | Job 5 | Amos 1 | Hebrews 5 |
| Day 6 | Genesis 6 | Job 6 | Amos 2 | Hebrews 6 |
| Day 7 | Genesis 7 | Job 7 | Amos 3 | Hebrews 7 |
| Day 8 | Genesis 8 | Job 8 | Amos 4 | Hebrews 8 |
| Day 9 | Genesis 9 | Job 9 | Amos 5:1-17 | Hebrews 9 |
| Day 10 | Genesis 10 | Job 10 | Amos 5:18-27 | Hebrews 10 |
| Day 11 | Genesis 11 | Job 11 | Amos 6 | Hebrews 11 |
| Day 12 | Genesis 12 | Job 12 | Amos 7 | Hebrews 12 |
| Day 13 | Genesis 13 | Job 13 | Amos 8 | Hebrews 13 |
| Day 14 | Genesis 14 | Job 14 | Amos 9 | Mark 1:1-18 |
| Day 15 | Genesis 15 | Job 15 | 2 Kings 15:32-38 | John 1:1-18 |
| Day 16 | Genesis 16 | Job 16 | 2 Chronicles 27 | John 1:19-34 |
| Day 17 | Genesis 17 | Job 17 | Hosea 1-2:1 | Matthew 1:1-7 |
| Day 18 | Genesis 18 | Job 18 | Hosea 2:2-23 | Matthew 3:1-12 |
| Day 19 | Genesis 19 | Job 19 | Hosea 3 | Luke 1:1-25 |
| Day 20 | Genesis 20 | Job 20 | Hosea 4 | Luke 1:26-38 |
| Day 21 | Genesis 21 | Job 21 | Hosea 5 | Luke 1:39-45 |

| Day | History | Teachings | Prophets | New Testament |
|-----|---------|-----------|----------|---------------|
| Day 22 | Genesis 22 | Job 22 | Hosea 6 | Luke 1:46-56 |
| Day 23 | Genesis 23 | Job 23 | Hosea 7 | Luke 1:57-66 |
| Day 24 | Genesis 24:1-21 | Job 24 | Hosea 8 | Luke 1:67-80 |
| Day 25 | Genesis 24:22-49 | Job 25 | Hosea 9 | Matthew 1:18-25 |
| Day 26 | Genesis 24:50-66 | Job 26 | Hosea 10 | Luke 2:1-7 |
| Day 27 | Genesis 25 | Job 27 | Hosea 11 | Luke 2:8-20 |
| Day 28 | Genesis 26 | Job 28 | Hosea 12 | 1 John 1 |
| Day 29 | Genesis 27:1-29 | Job 29 | Hosea 13 | 1 John 2 |
| Day 30 | Genesis 27:30-46 | Job 30 | Hosea 14 | 1 John 3 |
| Day 31 | Genesis 28 | Job 31 | 2 Kings 16 | 1 John 4 |
| Day 32 | Genesis 29 | Job 32 | 2 Chronicles 28:1-15 | 1 John 5 |
| Day 33 | Genesis 30 | Job 33 | 2 Chronicles 28:16-27 | Luke 3:1-20 |
| Day 34 | Genesis 31:1-21 | Job 34 | Micah 1 | Luke 3:23-38 |
| Day 35 | Genesis 31:22-42 | Job 35 | Micah 2 | Luke 2:21-38 |
| Day 36 | Genesis 31:43-55 | Job 36 | Micah 3 | Luke 2:39-52 |
| Day 37 | Genesis 32 | Job 37 | Micah 4 | 2 John |
| Day 38 | Genesis 33 | Job 38:1-24 | Micah 5 | 3 John |
| Day 39 | Genesis 24 | Job 38:25-41 | Micah 6 | Matthew 2 |
| Day 40 | Genesis 35 | Job 39 | Micah 7 | Luke 3:21-22 |
| Day 41 | Genesis 36 | Job 40 | 2 Kings 18:1-12 | Matthew 4 |
| Day 42 | Genesis 37 | Job 41 | 2 Kings 19:1-7 | Matthew 5:1-20 |
| Day 43 | Genesis 38 | Job 42 | 2 Kings 20 | Matthew 5:21-32 |
| Day 44 | Genesis 39 | Exodus 20 | 2 Chronicles 29:1-19 | Matthew 5:33-48 |
| Day 45 | Genesis 40 | Exodus 21 | 2 Chronicles 29:20-36 | Matthew 6 |

| Day | History | Teachings | Prophets | New Testament |
|-----|---------|-----------|----------|---------------|
| Day 46 | Genesis 41:1-36 | Exodus 22 | 2 Chronicles 30 | Matthew 7 |
| Day 47 | Genesis 41:37-57 | Exodus 23 | 2 Chronicles 31 | Matthew 8-9:1 |
| Day 48 | Genesis 42 | Exodus 24 | 2 Chronicles 32:1-19 | Matthew 9:2-26 |
| Day 49 | Genesis 43 | Exodus 25 | 2 Chronicles 32:20-33 | Matthew 9:27-38 |
| Day 50 | Genesis 44 | Exodus 26 | Isaiah 1 | Matthew 10 |
| Day 51 | Genesis 45 | Exodus 27 | Isaiah 2 | Matthew 11 |
| Day 52 | Genesis 46 | Exodus 28 | Isaiah 3 | Matthew 12:1-21 |
| Day 53 | Genesis 47 | Exodus 29 | Isaiah 4 | Matthew 12:22-37 |
| Day 54 | Genesis 48 | Exodus 30 | Isaiah 5 | Matthew 12:38-50 |
| Day 55 | Genesis 49 | Exodus 31 | Isaiah 6 | Matthew 13:1-17 |
| Day 56 | Genesis 50 | Exodus 32 | Isaiah 7 | Matthew 13:18-33 |
| Day 57 | Exodus 1 | Exodus 33 | Isaiah 8 | Matthew 14 |
| Day 58 | Exodus 2 | Exodus 34 | Isaiah 9 | Matthew 15 |
| Day 59 | Exodus 3 | Exodus 35 | Isaiah 10:1-19 | Matthew 16 |
| Day 60 | Exodus 4 | Exodus 36 | Isaiah 10:20-34 | Matthew 17 |
| Day 61 | Exodus 5 | Exodus 37 | Isaiah 11 | Matthew 18 |
| Day 62 | Exodus 6 | Exodus 38 | Isaiah 12 | Matthew 19 |
| Day 63 | Exodus 7 | Exodus 39 | Isaiah 13 | Matthew 20 |
| Day 64 | Exodus 8 | Exodus 40 | Isaiah 14 | Matthew 21:1-27 |
| Day 65 | Exodus 9 | Psalm 1 | Isaiah 15 | Matthew 21:28-45 |
| Day 66 | Exodus 10 | Psalm 2 | Isaiah 16 | Matthew 22:1-22 |
| Day 67 | Exodus 11 | Psalm 3 | Isaiah 17 | Matthew 22:23-46 |
| Day 68 | Exodus 12:1-28 | Psalm 4 | Isaiah 18 | Matthew 23 |
| Day 69 | Exodus 12:29-51 | Psalm 5 | Isaiah 19 | Matthew 24:1-31 |

| Day | History | Teachings | Prophets | New Testament |
|-----|---------|-----------|----------|---------------|
| Day 70 | Exodus 13 | Psalm 6 | Isaiah 20 | Matthew 24:32-51 |
| Day 71 | Exodus 14 | Psalm 7 | Isaiah 21 | Matthew 25:1-30 |
| Day 72 | Exodus 15 | Psalm 8 | Isaiah 22 | Matthew 25:31-46 |
| Day 73 | Exodus 16 | Psalm 9 | Isaiah 23 | 1 Corinthians 1 |
| Day 74 | Exodus 17 | Psalm 10 | Isaiah 24 | 1 Corinthians 2 |
| Day 75 | Exodus 18 | Psalm 11 | Isaiah 25 | 1 Corinthians 3 |
| Day 76 | Exodus 19 | Psalm 12 | Isaiah 26 | 1 Corinthians 4 |
| Day 77 | Numbers 10:11-35 | Psalm 13 | Isaiah 27 | 1 Corinthians 5 |
| Day 78 | Numbers 11 | Psalm 14 | Isaiah 28 | 1 Corinthians 6 |
| Day 79 | Numbers 12 | Psalm 15 | Isaiah 29 | 1 Corinthians 7:1-24 |
| Day 80 | Numbers 13 | Psalm 16 | Isaiah 30:1-17 | 1 Corinthians 7:25-39 |
| Day 81 | Numbers 14 | Psalm 17 | Isaiah 30:18-33 | 1 Corinthians 8 |
| Day 82 | Numbers 16 | Psalm 18:1-25 | Isaiah 31 | 1 Corinthians 9 |
| Day 83 | Numbers 17 | Psalm 18:25-50 | Isaiah 32 | 1 Corinthians 10-11:1 |
| Day 84 | Numbers 20 | Psalm 19 | Isaiah 33 | 1 Corinthians 11:2-34 |
| Day 85 | Numbers 21 | Psalm 20 | Isaiah 34 | 1 Corinthians 12 |
| Day 86 | Numbers 22:1-40 | Psalm 21 | Isaiah 35 | 1 Corinthians 13 |
| Day 87 | Numbers 22:41-23:30 | Psalm 22 | Isaiah 36 | 1 Corinthians 14:1-25 |
| Day 88 | Numbers 24 | Psalm 23 | Isaiah 37:1-13 | 1 Corinthians 14:26-50 |

| Day | History | Teachings | Prophets | New Testament |
|---|---|---|---|---|
| Day 89 | Numbers 25 | Psalm 24 | Isaiah 37:14-35 | 1 Corinthians 15:1-11 |
| Day 90 | Numbers 27 | Psalm 25 | Isaiah 37:36-38 | 1 Corinthians 15:12-34 |
| Day 91 | Numbers 31:1-24 | Psalm 26 | Isaiah 38 | 1 Corinthians 15:35-58 |
| Day 92 | Numbers 31:25-54 | Psalm 27 | Isaiah 39 | 1 Corinthians 16 |
| Day 93 | Numbers 32 | Psalm 28 | 2 Kings 22 | 1 Peter 1 |
| Day 94 | Numbers 33:1-37 | Psalm 29 | 2 Kings 23:1-20 | 1 Peter 2 |
| Day 95 | Numbers 33:38-56 | Psalm 30 | 2 Kings 23:21-30 | 1 Peter 3 |
| Day 96 | Deuteronomy 1 | Psalm 31 | Zephaniah 1 | 1 Peter 4 |
| Day 97 | Deuteronomy 2 | Psalm 32 | Zephaniah 2 | 1 Peter 5 |
| Day 98 | Deuteronomy 3 | Psalm 33 | Zephaniah 3 | 2 Peter 1 |
| Day 99 | Deuteronomy 4:1-31 | Psalm 34 | 2 Chronicles 34:1-21 | 2 Peter 2 |
| Day 100 | Deuteronomy 4:32-49 | Psalm 35 | 2 Chronicles 34:22-33 | 2 Peter 3 |
| Day 101 | Deuteronomy 31:1-29 | Psalm 36 | 2 Chronicles 35:1-19 | Philemon |
| Day 102 | Deuteronomy 31:30-32:52 | Psalm 37 | 2 Chronicles 35:20-27 | Jude |
| Day 103 | Deuteronomy 33 | Psalm 38 | 2 Chronicles 36:1-10 | Mark 1:12-28 |
| Day 104 | Deuteronomy 34 | Psalm 39 | 2 Kings 23:31-37 | Mark 1:29-45 |
| Day 105 | Joshua 1 | Psalm 40 | 2 Kings 24:1-17 | Mark 2 |
| Day 106 | Joshua 2 | Psalm 41 | Jeremiah 1 | Mark 3 |
| Day 107 | Joshua 3 | Leviticus 1 | Jeremiah 2:1-22 | Mark 4:1-20 |
| Day 108 | Joshua 4 | Leviticus 2 | Jeremiah 2:23-37 | Mark 4:21-41 |

| Day | History | Teachings | Prophets | New Testament |
|-----|---------|-----------|----------|---------------|
| Day 109 | Joshua 5 | Leviticus 3 | Jeremiah 3:1-5 | Mark 5:1-20 |
| Day 110 | Joshua 6 | Leviticus 4 | Jeremiah 3:6-25 | Mark 5:21-43 |
| Day 111 | Joshua 7 | Leviticus 5 | Jeremiah 4:1-4 | Mark 6:1-29 |
| Day 112 | Joshua 8 | Leviticus 6 | Jeremiah 4:5-31 | Mark 6:30-56 |
| Day 113 | Joshua 9 | Leviticus 7 | Jeremiah 5 | Mark 7 |
| Day 114 | Joshua 10 | Leviticus 8 | Jeremiah 6 | Mark 8-9:1 |
| Day 115 | Joshua 11 | Leviticus 9 | Jeremiah 7:1-15 | Mark 9:2-29 |
| Day 116 | Joshua 12 | Leviticus 10 | Jeremiah 7:16-26 | Mark 9:30-49 |
| Day 117 | Joshua 13 | Leviticus 11:1-23 | Jeremiah 7:27-8:3 | Mark 10:1-31 |
| Day 118 | Joshua 14 | Leviticus 11:24-47 | Jeremiah 8:4-22 | Mark 10:32-52 |
| Day 119 | Joshua 15:1-19 | Leviticus 12 | Jeremiah 9 | Mark 11 |
| Day 120 | Joshua 15:20-63 | Leviticus 13:1-28 | Jeremiah 10 | Mark 12:1-27 |
| Day 121 | Joshua 16 | Leviticus 13:29-59 | Jeremiah 11 | Mark 12:28-44 |
| Day 122 | Joshua 17 | Leviticus 14:1-32 | Jeremiah 12 | Mark 13 |
| Day 123 | Joshua 18 | Leviticus 14:33-57 | Jeremiah 13 | Matthew 26:1-16 |
| Day 124 | Joshua 19 | Leviticus 15 | Jeremiah 14 | Matthew 26:17-30 |
| Day 125 | Joshua 20 | Leviticus 16 | Jeremiah 15 | Matthew 26:57-75 |
| Day 126 | Joshua 21 | Leviticus 17 | Jeremiah 16 | Matthew 27:1-14 |
| Day 127 | Joshua 22 | Leviticus 18 | Jeremiah 17 | Matthew 27:15-31 |
| Day 128 | Joshua 23 | Leviticus 19 | Jeremiah 18 | Matthew 27:32-44 |
| Day 129 | Joshua 24 | Leviticus 20 | Jeremiah 19 | Matthew 27:45-66 |

| Day | History | Teachings | Prophets | New Testament |
|---|---|---|---|---|
| Day 130 | Judges 1 | Leviticus 21 | Jeremiah 20 | Mark 14:1-21 |
| Day 131 | Judges 2 | Leviticus 22 | Jeremiah 21 | Mark 14:22-31 |
| Day 132 | Judges 3 | Leviticus 23:1-22 | Jeremiah 22 | Mark 14:32-51 |
| Day 133 | Judges 4 | Leviticus 23:23-44 | Jeremiah 23:1-22 | Mark 14:52-72 |
| Day 134 | Judges 5 | Leviticus 24 | Jeremiah 23:23-40 | Mark 15:1-20 |
| Day 135 | Judges 6 | Leviticus 25:1-17 | Jeremiah 24 | Mark 15:21-32 |
| Day 136 | Judges 7 | Leviticus 25:18-38 | Jeremiah 25:1-14 | Luke 22:1-23 |
| Day 137 | Judges 8 | Leviticus 25:39-55 | Jeremiah 25:15-38 | Luke 22:24-38 |
| Day 138 | Judges 9:1-21 | Leviticus 26:1-26 | Jeremiah 26 | Luke 22:39-53 |
| Day 139 | Judges 9:22-41 | Leviticus 26:27-46 | Jeremiah 27 | Luke 22:54-71 |
| Day 140 | Judges 9:42-57 | Leviticus 27 | Jeremiah 28 | Luke 23:1-12 |
| Day 141 | Judges 10 | Psalm 42 | Jeremiah 29:1-23 | Luke 23:13-25 |
| Day 142 | Judges 11 | Psalm 43 | Jeremiah 29:24-32 | Luke 23:26-43 |
| Day 143 | Judges 12 | Psalm 44 | Jeremiah 30 | Luke 23:44-56 |
| Day 144 | Judges 13 | Psalm 45 | Jeremiah 31:1-14 | John 17 |
| Day 145 | Judges 14 | Psalm 46 | Jeremiah 31:15-30 | John 18:1-24 |
| Day 146 | Judges 15 | Psalm 47 | Jeremiah 31:31-40 | John 18:25-38a |
| Day 147 | Judges 16 | Psalm 48 | Jeremiah 32:1-25 | John 18:38b-19:16 |
| Day 148 | Judges 17 | Psalm 49 | Jeremiah 32:26-44 | John 19:17-42 |
| Day 149 | Judges 18 | Psalm 50 | Jeremiah 33 | Matthew 28 |

| Day | History | Teachings | Prophets | New Testament |
|---|---|---|---|---|
| Day 150 | Judges 19 | Psalm 51 | Jeremiah 34 | Mark 16 |
| Day 151 | Judges 20:1-23 | Psalm 52 | Jeremiah 35 | Luke 24:1-12 |
| Day 152 | Judges 20:24-48 | Psalm 53 | Jeremiah 36:1-19 | John 20:1-18 |
| Day 153 | Judges 21 | Psalm 54 | Jeremiah 36:20-32 | 1 Timothy 1 |
| Day 154 | Ruth 1 | Psalm 55 | Jeremiah 33 | 1 Timothy 2 |
| Day 155 | Ruth 2 | Psalm 56 | Jeremiah 34 | 1 Timothy 3 |
| Day 156 | Ruth 3 | Psalm 57 | Jeremiah 35 | 1 Timothy 4 |
| Day 157 | Ruth 4 | Psalm 58 | Jeremiah 36:1-19 | 1 Timothy 5 |
| Day 158 | 1 Samuel 1 | Psalm 59 | Jeremiah 36:20-32 | 1 Timothy 6 |
| Day 159 | 1 Samuel 2 | Psalm 60 | Jeremiah 37 | 2 Timothy 1 |
| Day 160 | 1 Samuel 3 | Psalm 61 | Jeremiah 38 | 2 Timothy 2 |
| Day 161 | 1 Samuel 4 | Psalm 62 | Jeremiah 39 | 2 Timothy 3 |
| Day 162 | 1 Samuel 5 | Psalm 63 | Jeremiah 40 | 2 Timothy 4 |
| Day 163 | 1 Samuel 6 | Psalm 64 | Jeremiah 41 | Luke 4:1-36 |
| Day 164 | 1 Samuel 7 | Psalm 65 | Jeremiah 42 | Luke 4:31-44 |
| Day 165 | 1 Samuel 8 | Psalm 66 | Jeremiah 43 | Luke 5:1-26 |
| Day 166 | 1 Samuel 9 | Psalm 67 | Jeremiah 44:1-20 | Luke 5:27-39 |
| Day 167 | 1 Samuel 10 | Psalm 68 | Jeremiah 44:21-30 | Luke 6:1-26 |
| Day 168 | 1 Samuel 11 | Psalm 69 | Jeremiah 45 | Luke 6:27-49 |
| Day 169 | 1 Samuel 12 | Psalm 70 | Jeremiah 46:1-12 | Luke 7:1-35 |
| Day 170 | 1 Samuel 13 | Psalm 71 | Jeremiah 46:13-28 | Luke 7:36-50 |
| Day 171 | 1 Samuel 14:1-23 | Psalm 72 | Jeremiah 47 | Luke 8:1-17 |
| Day 172 | 1 Samuel 14:24-52 | Proverbs 1 | Jeremiah 48:1-13 | Luke 8:18-39 |
| Day 173 | 1 Samuel 15 | Proverbs 2 | Jeremiah 48:14-27 | Luke 8:40-55 |

| Day | History | Teachings | Prophets | New Testament |
|---|---|---|---|---|
| Day 174 | 1 Samuel 16 | Proverbs 3 | Jeremiah 48:28-47 | Luke 9:1-20 |
| Day 175 | 1 Samuel 17:1-23 | Proverbs 4 | Jeremiah 49:1-22 | Luke 9:21-36 |
| Day 176 | 1 Samuel 17:24-40 | Proverbs 5 | Jeremiah 49:23-39 | Luke 9:37-50 |
| Day 177 | 1 Samuel 17:41-58 | Proverbs 6 | Jeremiah 50:1-16 | Luke 9:50-62 |
| Day 178 | 1 Samuel 18 | Proverbs 7 | Jeremiah 50:17-32 | Luke 10:1-24 |
| Day 179 | 1 Samuel 19 | Proverbs 8 | Jeremiah 51:1-10 | Luke 10:25-42 |
| Day 180 | 1 Samuel 20 | Proverbs 9 | Jeremiah 51:11-23 | Luke 11:1-23 |
| Day 181 | 1 Samuel 21 | Proverbs 10 | Jeremiah 51:45-64 | Luke 11:24-36 |
| Day 182 | 1 Samuel 22 | Proverbs 11 | Jeremiah 52:1-16 | Luke 11:37-54 |
| Day 183 | 1 Samuel 23 | Proverbs 12 | Jeremiah 52:17-34 | Luke 12:1-21 |
| Day 184 | 1 Samuel 24 | Proverbs 13 | 2 Kings 24:18-25:21 | Luke 12:22-40 |
| Day 185 | 1 Samuel 25:1-22 | Proverbs 14 | 2 Kings 25:22-30 | Luke 12:41-59 |
| Day 186 | 1 Samuel 25:23-44 | Proverbs 15 | 2 Chronicles 36:11-21 | Luke 13 |
| Day 187 | 1 Samuel 26 | Proverbs 16 | Lamentations 1 | Luke 14 |
| Day 188 | 1 Samuel 27 | Proverbs 17 | Lamentations 2 | Luke 15 |
| Day 189 | 1 Samuel 28 | Proverbs 18 | Lamentations 3:1-18 | Luke 16 |
| Day 190 | 1 Samuel 29 | Proverbs 19 | Lamentations 3:19-36 | Luke 17 |
| Day 191 | 1 Samuel 30 | Proverbs 20 | Lamentations 3:37-48 | Luke 18 |
| Day 192 | 1 Samuel 31 | Proverbs 21 | Lamentations 3:49-66 | Luke 19:1-27 |

| Day | History | Teachings | Prophets | New Testament |
|---|---|---|---|---|
| Day 193 | 2 Samuel 1 | Proverbs 22 | Lamentations 4 | Luke 19:28-48 |
| Day 194 | 2 Samuel 2 | Proverbs 23 | Lamentations 5 | Luke 20:1-26 |
| Day 195 | 2 Samuel 3 | Proverbs 24 | Habakkuk 1 | Luke 20:27-47 |
| Day 196 | 2 Samuel 4 | Proverbs 25 | Habakkuk 2 | Luke 21 |
| Day 197 | 2 Samuel 5 | Proverbs 26 | Habakkuk 3 | Luke 24:13-35 |
| Day 198 | 2 Samuel 6 | Proverbs 27 | Ezekiel 1 | Luke 24:36-53 |
| Day 199 | 2 Samuel 7 | Proverbs 28 | Ezekiel 2 | Acts 1 |
| Day 200 | 2 Samuel 8 | Proverbs 29 | Ezekiel 3 | Acts 2:1-36 |
| Day 201 | 2 Samuel 9 | Proverbs 30 | Ezekiel 4 | Acts 2:37-47 |
| Day 202 | 2 Samuel 10 | Proverbs 31 | Ezekiel 5 | Acts 3 |
| Day 203 | 2 Samuel 11 | Psalm 73 | Ezekiel 6 | Acts 4 |
| Day 204 | 2 Samuel 12 | Psalm 74 | Ezekiel 7 | Acts 5 |
| Day 205 | 2 Samuel 13 | Psalm 75 | Ezekiel 8 | Acts 6 |
| Day 206 | 2 Samuel 14 | Psalm 76 | Ezekiel 9 | Acts 7:1-29 |
| Day 207 | 2 Samuel 15 | Psalm 77 | Ezekiel 10 | Acts 7:30-53 |
| Day 208 | 2 Samuel 16 | Psalm 78:1-31 | Ezekiel 11 | Acts 7:54-8:1a |
| Day 209 | 2 Samuel 17 | Psalm 78:32-72 | Ezekiel 12 | Acts 8:1b-35 |
| Day 210 | 2 Samuel 18 | Psalm 79 | Ezekiel 13 | Acts 8:26-40 |
| Day 211 | 2 Samuel 19 | Psalm 80 | Ezekiel 14 | Acts 9:1-25 |
| Day 212 | 2 Samuel 20 | Psalm 81 | Ezekiel 15 | Acts 9:26-43 |
| Day 213 | 2 Samuel 21 | Psalm 82 | Ezekiel 16:1-22 | Acts 10:1-33 |
| Day 214 | 2 Samuel 22 | Psalm 83 | Ezekiel 16:23-52 | Acts 10:34-48 |
| Day 215 | 2 Samuel 23 | Psalm 84 | Ezekiel 16:53-63 | Acts 11 |
| Day 216 | 2 Samuel 24 | Psalm 85 | Ezekiel 17 | Acts 12 |
| Day 217 | 1 Kings 1:1-27 | Psalm 86 | Ezekiel 18 | Acts 13:1-25 |
| Day 218 | 1 Kings 1:28-53 | Psalm 87 | Ezekiel 19 | Acts 13:26-52 |
| Day 219 | 1 Kings 2 | Psalm 88 | Ezekiel 20:1-32 | Acts 14 |

| Day | History | Teachings | Prophets | New Testament |
|---|---|---|---|---|
| Day 220 | 1 Kings 3 | Psalm 89:1-18 | Ezekiel 20:33-49 | Acts 15:1-21 |
| Day 221 | 1 Kings 4 | Psalm 89:19-37 | Ezekiel 21 | Acts 15:22-41 |
| Day 222 | 1 Kings 5 | Psalm 89:38-52 | Ezekiel 22 | Acts 16:1-15 |
| Day 223 | 1 Kings 6 | Numbers 1 | Ezekiel 23:1-21 | Acts 16:16-24 |
| Day 224 | 1 Kings 7:1-22 | Numbers 2 | Ezekiel 23:22-49 | Acts 16:25-41 |
| Day 225 | 1 Kings 7:23-51 | Numbers 3 | Ezekiel 24 | Acts 17 |
| Day 226 | 1 Kings 8:1-13 | Numbers 4 | Ezekiel 25 | Acts 18 |
| Day 227 | 1 Kings 8:14-36 | Numbers 5 | Ezekiel 26 | Acts 19 |
| Day 228 | 1 Kings 8:37-53 | Numbers 6 | Ezekiel 27 | Acts 20 |
| Day 229 | 1 Kings 8:54-66 | Numbers 7:1-23 | Ezekiel 28 | Acts 21 |
| Day 230 | 1 Kings 9 | Numbers 7:24-47 | Ezekiel 29 | Acts 22:1-29 |
| Day 231 | 1 Kings 10 | Numbers 7:48-71 | Ezekiel 30 | Acts 22:29-23:35 |
| Day 232 | 1 Kings 11 | Numbers 7:72-90 | Ezekiel 31 | Acts 24 |
| Day 233 | 1 Kings 12 | Numbers 8 | Ezekiel 32 | Acts 25 |
| Day 234 | 1 Kings 13 | Numbers 9 | Ezekiel 33 | Acts 26 |
| Day 235 | 1 Kings 14 | Numbers 10:1-10 | Ezekiel 34 | Acts 27:1-12 |
| Day 236 | 1 Kings 15 | Numbers 15 | Ezekiel 35 | Acts 27:13-44 |
| Day 237 | 1 Kings 16 | Numbers 18 | Ezekiel 36:1-15 | Acts 28 |
| Day 238 | 1 Kings 17 | Numbers 19 | Ezekiel 36:16-38 | Ephesians 1 |
| Day 239 | 1 Kings 18 | Numbers 26 | Ezekiel 37 | Ephesians 2 |
| Day 240 | 1 Kings 19 | Numbers 28 | Ezekiel 38 | Ephesians 3 |

| Day | History | Teachings | Prophets | New Testament |
|-----|---------|-----------|----------|---------------|
| Day 241 | 1 Kings 20 | Numbers 29 | Ezekiel 39 | Ephesians 4-5:2 |
| Day 242 | 1 Kings 21 | Numbers 30 | Ezekiel 40:1-23 | Ephesians 5:3-33 |
| Day 243 | 1 Kings 22 | Numbers 34 | Ezekiel 40:24-47 | Ephesians 6 |
| Day 244 | 2 Kings 1 | Numbers 35 | Ezekiel 40:48-41:26 | Philippians 1 |
| Day 245 | 2 Kings 2 | Numbers 36 | Ezekiel 42 | Philippians 2-3:1a |
| Day 246 | 2 Kings 3 | Ecclesiastes 1 | Ezekiel 43 | Philippians 3:1b-4:1 |
| Day 247 | 2 Kings 4 | Ecclesiastes 2 | Ezekiel 44 | Philippians 4:2-23 |
| Day 248 | 2 Kings 5 | Ecclesiastes 3 | Ezekiel 45 | Colossians 1:1-23 |
| Day 249 | 2 Kings 6 | Ecclesiastes 4 | Ezekiel 46 | Colossians 1:24-2:23 |
| Day 250 | 2 Kings 7 | Ecclesiastes 5 | Ezekiel 47 | Colossians 3-4:1 |
| Day 251 | 2 Kings 8 | Ecclesiastes 6 | Ezekiel 48 | Colossians 4:2-18 |
| Day 252 | 2 Kings 9 | Ecclesiastes 7 | Nahum 1 | 2 Corinthians 1-2:4 |
| Day 253 | 2 Kings 10 | Ecclesiastes 8 | Nahum 2 | 2 Corinthians 2:5-17 |
| Day 254 | 2 Kings 11 | Ecclesiastes 9 | Nahum 3 | 2 Corinthians 3 |
| Day 255 | 2 Kings 12 | Ecclesiastes 10 | Jonah 1 | 2 Corinthians 4:1-15 |
| Day 256 | 2 Kings 13 | Ecclesiastes 11 | Jonah 2 | 2 Corinthians 4:16-5:10 |
| Day 257 | 2 Kings 14 | Ecclesiastes 12 | Jonah 3 | 2 Corinthians 5:11-6:13 |
| Day 258 | 2 Kings 15 | Deuterono-my 5 | Jonah 4 | 2 Corinthians 6:14-7:1 |
| Day 259 | 2 Kings 16 | Deuterono-my 6 | 2 Chronicles 36:22-23 | 2 Corinthians 7:2-16 |

| Day | History | Teachings | Prophets | New Testament |
|-----|---------|-----------|----------|---------------|
| Day 260 | 2 Kings 17 | Deuteronomy 7 | Ezra 1 | 2 Corinthians 8 |
| Day 261 | 2 Kings 18 | Deuteronomy 8 | Isaiah 40 | 2 Corinthians 9 |
| Day 262 | 2 Kings 19 | Deuteronomy 9 | Isaiah 41:1-16 | 2 Corinthians 10 |
| Day 263 | 2 Kings 20 | Deuteronomy 10 | Isaiah 41:17-29 | 2 Corinthians 11 |
| Day 264 | 2 Kings 21 | Deuteronomy 11 | Isaiah 42:1-20 | 2 Corinthians 12 |
| Day 265 | 2 Kings 22 | Deuteronomy 12 | Isaiah 42:21-25 | 2 Corinthians 13 |
| Day 266 | 2 Kings 23 | Deuteronomy 13 | Isaiah 43:1-13 | Galatians 1 |
| Day 267 | 2 Kings 24 | Deuteronomy 14 | Isaiah 43:14-28 | Galatians 2 |
| Day 268 | 2 Kings 25 | Deuteronomy 15 | Isaiah 44:1-20 | Galatians 3:1-18 |
| Day 269 | 1 Chronicles 1 | Deuteronomy 16 | Isaiah 44:21-28 | Galatians 3:19-4:7 |
| Day 270 | 1 Chronicles 2 | Deuteronomy 17 | Isaiah 45 | Galatians 4:8-5:1 |
| Day 271 | 1 Chronicles 3 | Deuteronomy 18 | Isaiah 46 | Galatians 5:2-26 |
| Day 272 | 1 Chronicles 4 | Deuteronomy 19 | Isaiah 47 | Galatians 6 |
| Day 273 | 1 Chronicles 5 | Deuteronomy 20 | Isaiah 48 | Romans 1 |
| Day 274 | 1 Chronicles 6 | Deuteronomy 21 | Isaiah 49:1-7 | Romans 2:1-3:8 |
| Day 275 | 1 Chronicles 7 | Deuteronomy 22 | Isaiah 49:8-26 | Romans 3:9-31 |
| Day 276 | 1 Chronicles 8 | Deuteronomy 23 | Isaiah 50 | Romans 4 |

| Day | History | Teachings | Prophets | New Testament |
|---|---|---|---|---|
| Day 277 | 1 Chronicles 9 | Deuteronomy 24 | Isaiah 51 | Romans 5 |
| Day 278 | 1 Chronicles 10 | Deuteronomy 25 | Isaiah 52 | Romans 6 |
| Day 279 | 1 Chronicles 11 | Deuteronomy 26 | Isaiah 53 | Romans 7 |
| Day 280 | 1 Chronicles 12 | Deuteronomy 27 | Isaiah 54 | Romans 8:1-17 |
| Day 281 | 1 Chronicles 13 | Deuteronomy 28:1:19 | Isaiah 55 | Romans 8:17-39 |
| Day 282 | 1 Chronicles 14 | Deuteronomy 28:20-44 | Joel 1 | Romans 9:1-29 |
| Day 283 | 1 Chronicles 15 | Deuteronomy 28:45-29:1 | Joel 2:1-17 | Romans 9:30-10:21 |
| Day 284 | 1 Chronicles 16 | Deuteronomy 29:2-29 | Joel 2:18-32 | Romans 11 |
| Day 285 | 1 Chronicles 17 | Deuteronomy 30 | Joel 3 | Romans 12 |
| Day 286 | 1 Chronicles 18 | Song of Songs 1 | Obadiah | Romans 13 |
| Day 287 | 1 Chronicles 19 | Song of Songs 2 | Daniel 1 | Romans 14 |
| Day 288 | 1 Chronicles 20 | Song of Songs 3 | Daniel 2:1-16 | Romans 15 |
| Day 289 | 1 Chronicles 21 | Song of Songs 4 | Daniel 2:17-30 | Romans 16 |
| Day 290 | 1 Chronicles 22 | Song of Songs 5 | Daniel 2:31-49 | Titus 1 |
| Day 291 | 1 Chronicles 23 | Song of Songs 6 | Daniel 3:1-18 | Titus 2 |
| Day 292 | 1 Chronicles 24 | Song of Songs 7 | Daniel 3:19-30 | Titus 3 |
| Day 293 | 1 Chronicles 25 | Song of Songs 8 | Daniel 4:1-18 | James 1 |

| Day | History | Teachings | Prophets | New Testament |
|---|---|---|---|---|
| Day 294 | 1 Chronicles 26 | Psalm 90 | Daniel 4:19-27 | James 2 |
| Day 295 | 1 Chronicles 27 | Psalm 91 | Daniel 4:28-37 | James 3 |
| Day 296 | 1 Chronicles 28 | Psalm 92 | Daniel 5:1-12 | James 4 |
| Day 297 | 1 Chronicles 29 | Psalm 93 | Daniel 5:13-30 | James 5 |
| Day 298 | 2 Chronicles 1 | Psalm 94 | Daniel 6 | John 1:35-51 |
| Day 299 | 2 Chronicles 2 | Psalm 95 | Esther 1 | John 2 |
| Day 300 | 2 Chronicles 3 | Psalm 96 | Esther 2 | John 3 |
| Day 301 | 2 Chronicles 4 | Psalm 97 | Esther 3 | John 4:1-26 |
| Day 302 | 2 Chronicles 5 | Psalm 98 | Esther 4 | John 4:27-54 |
| Day 303 | 2 Chronicles 6 | Psalm 99 | Esther 5 | John 5:1-29 |
| Day 304 | 2 Chronicles 7 | Psalm 100 | Esther 6 | John 5:30-47 |
| Day 305 | 2 Chronicles 8 | Psalm 101 | Esther 7 | John 6:1-21 |
| Day 306 | 2 Chronicles 9 | Psalm 102 | Esther 8 | John 6:22-40 |
| Day 307 | 2 Chronicles 10 | Psalm 103 | Esther 9:1-17 | John 6:41-59 |
| Day 308 | 2 Chronicles 11 | Psalm 104 | Esther 9:18-28 | John 6:60-71 |
| Day 309 | 2 Chronicles 12 | Psalm 105 | Esther 9:29-10:3 | John 7:1-24 |
| Day 310 | 2 Chronicles 13 | Psalm 106:1-23 | Isaiah 56 | John 7:25-36 |
| Day 311 | 2 Chronicles 14 | Psalm 106:24-48 | Isaiah 57 | John 7:37-52 |
| Day 312 | 2 Chronicles 15 | Psalm 107 | Isaiah 58 | John 7:53-8:30 |
| Day 313 | 2 Chronicles 16 | Psalm 108 | Isaiah 59 | John 8:31-59 |
| Day 314 | 2 Chronicles 17 | Psalm 109 | Isaiah 60 | John 9 |
| Day 315 | 2 Chronicles 18 | Psalm 110 | Isaiah 61 | John 10 |
| Day 316 | 2 Chronicles 19 | Psalm 111 | Isaiah 62 | John 11:1-27 |
| Day 317 | 2 Chronicles 20 | Psalm 112 | Isaiah 63 | John 11:28-57 |

| Day | History | Teachings | Prophets | New Testament |
|---|---|---|---|---|
| Day 318 | 2 Chronicles 21 | Psalm 113 | Isaiah 64 | John 12:1-19 |
| Day 319 | 2 Chronicles 22 | Psalm 114 | Isaiah 65:1-16 | John 12:20-36a |
| Day 320 | 2 Chronicles 23 | Psalm 115 | Isaiah 65:17-25 | John 12:36b-50 |
| Day 321 | 2 Chronicles 24 | Psalm 116 | Isaiah 66:1-13 | John 13 |
| Day 322 | 2 Chronicles 25 | Psalm 117 | Isaiah 66:14-24 | John 14 |
| Day 323 | 2 Chronicles 26 | Psalm 118 | Zechariah 1 | John 15-16:4a |
| Day 324 | 2 Chronicles 27 | Psalm 119:1-16 | Zechariah 2 | John 16:4b-33 |
| Day 325 | 2 Chronicles 28 | Psalm 119:17-32 | Zechariah 3 | John 20:19-31 |
| Day 326 | 2 Chronicles 29 | Psalm 119:33-48 | Zechariah 4 | John 21 |
| Day 327 | 2 Chronicles 30 | Psalm 119:49-64 | Zechariah 5 | 1 Thessalonians 1 |
| Day 328 | 2 Chronicles 31 | Psalm 119:65-80 | Zechariah 6 | 1 Thessalonians 2:1-16 |
| Day 329 | 2 Chronicles 32 | Psalm 119:81-96 | Zechariah 7 | 1 Thessalonians 2:17-3:13 |
| Day 330 | 2 Chronicles 33 | Psalm 119:97-112 | Zechariah 8 | 1 Thessalonians 4:1-12 |
| Day 331 | 2 Chronicles 34 | Psalm 119:113-128 | Zechariah 9 | 1 Thessalonians 4:13-5:11 |
| Day 332 | 2 Chronicles 35 | Psalm 119:129-144 | Zechariah 10 | 1 Thessalonians 5:12-28 |
| Day 333 | 2 Chronicles 36 | Psalm 119:145-160 | Zechariah 11 | 2 Thessalonians 1 |
| Day 334 | Ezra 1 | Psalm 119:161-176 | Zechariah 12-13:1 | 2 Thessalonians 2 |

| Day | History | Teachings | Prophets | New Testament |
|---|---|---|---|---|
| Day 335 | Ezra 2 | Psalm 120 | Zechariah 13:2-9 | 2 Thessalonians 3 |
| Day 336 | Ezra 3 | Psalm 121 | Zechariah 14 | Revelation 1 |
| Day 337 | Ezra 4 | Psalm 122 | Nehemiah 7:73b-8:18 | Revelation 2:1-11 |
| Day 338 | Ezra 5 | Psalm 123 | Nehemiah 9:1-25 | Revelation 2:12-29 |
| Day 339 | Ezra 6 | Psalm 124 | Nehemiah 9:26-37 | Revelation 3:1-6 |
| Day 340 | Ezra 7 | Psalm 125 | Nehemiah 10:28-39 | Revelation 3:7-13 |
| Day 341 | Ezra 8 | Psalm 126 | Haggai 1 | Revelation 3:14-22 |
| Day 342 | Ezra 9 | Psalm 127 | Haggai 2:1-9 | Revelation 4 |
| Day 343 | Ezra 10 | Psalm 128 | Ezra 3:8-4:5 | Revelation 5 |
| Day 344 | Nehemiah 1 | Psalm 129 | Ezra 4:6-24 | Revelation 6 |
| Day 345 | Nehemiah 2 | Psalm 130 | Haggai 2:10-19 | Revelation 7 |
| Day 346 | Nehemiah 3 | Psalm 131 | Ezra 5 | Revelation 8:1-5 |
| Day 347 | Nehemiah 4 | Psalm 132 | Ezra 6 | Revelation 8:6-9:21 |
| Day 348 | Nehemiah 5 | Psalm 133 | Haggai 2:21-23 | Revelation 10 |
| Day 349 | Nehemiah 6 | Psalm 134 | Ezra 8:15-30 | Revelation 11 |
| Day 350 | Nehemiah 7 | Psalm 135 | Nehemiah 12:44-47 | Revelation 12:1-7 |
| Day 351 | Nehemiah 8 | Psalm 136 | Malachi 1:1-2:9 | Revelation 12:8-13:18 |
| Day 352 | Nehemiah 9 | Psalm 137 | Malachi 2:10-17 | Revelation 14 |
| Day 353 | Nehemiah 10 | Psalm 138 | Malachi 3 | Revelation 15 |
| Day 354 | Nehemiah 11 | Psalm 139 | Malachi 4 | Revelation 16 |
| Day 355 | Nehemiah 12 | Psalm 140 | Daniel 7:1-14 | Revelation 17 |
| Day 356 | Nehemiah 13 | Psalm 141 | Daniel 7:15-28 | Revelation 18 |
| Day 357 | Esther 1 | Psalm 142 | Daniel 8:1-14 | Revelation 19 |

| Day | History | Teachings | Prophets | New Testament |
|-----|---------|-----------|----------|---------------|
| Day 358 | Esther 2 | Psalm 143 | Daniel 8:15-27 | Revelation 20 |
| Day 359 | Esther 3 | Psalm 144 | Daniel 9:1-19 | Genesis 1:1-23 |
| Day 360 | Esther 4 | Psalm 145 | Daniel 9:20-27 | Genesis 1:24-2:4a |
| Day 361 | Esther 5 | Psalm 146 | Daniel 10:1-17 | Genesis 2:4b-25 |
| Day 362 | Esther 6 | Psalm 147 | Daniel 10:18-11:13 | Revelation 21:1-8 |
| Day 363 | Esther 7 | Psalm 148 | Daniel 11:14-28 | Revelation 21:9-26 |
| Day 364 | Esther 8 | Psalm 149 | Daniel 11:29-45 | Revelation 22:1-7 |
| Day 365 | Esther 9-10 | Psalm 150 | Daniel 12 | Revelation 22:8-21 |

# Bibliography

Brueggemann, Walter. *The Message of the Psalms: A Theological Commentary*. Minneapolis, MN: Augsburg Fortress Press, 1984.

Claiborne, Shane, Jonathan Wilson-Hartgrove, and Enuma Okoro. *Common Prayer: A Liturgy for Ordinary Radicals*. Grand Rapids, MI: Zondervan, 2010.

Cron, Ian Morgan, and Suzanne Stabile. *The Road Back to You: An Enneagram Journey to Self-Discovery*. Downers Grove, IL: InterVarsity Press, 2016.

Freeman, Wilson C. "The Logan Act: An Overview of a Sometimes Forgotten 18th Century Law," Congressional Research Service, https://fas.org/sgp/crs/misc/LSB10058.pdf, accessed August 11, 2020.

Friedman, Edwin H. "The Bridge," in *Friedman's Fables*. New York: Guilford Press, 1990.

Lewis, C.S. "Letter to Mrs. D. Jessup, March 26, 1944," in *The C.S. Lewis Bible*. New York: HarperOne, 2010.

Rigg, James Harrison. *The Living Wesley*. London: Charles H. Kelly, 1891.

Santos, Jason Brian. *A Community Called Taizé: A Story of Prayer, Worship and Reconciliation*. Downers Grove, IL: IVP Books, 2008.

Taizé, "Aber du weißt den Weg für mich," *Music of Unity and Peace*. Berlin: Deutsche Grammophon, 2015.

Watts, Isaac. "Marching to Zion," in *The United Methodist Hymnal*. Nashville: United Methodist Publishing House, 1989.

Weil, Simone, trans. Emma Craufurd. *Waiting for God*. New York: Harper Perennial, 1951.

# About the Author

Growing up in Rome, Georgia, the Reverend Doctor Ted Goshorn never expected to become a pastor. Having first pursued a career in higher education, Ted found a calling for helping individuals grow in their faith and churches to transform their communities. As a result of that call, Ted joined the ministry as an ordained United Methodist elder in the South Georgia Annual Conference. Since June 2022, he has served Mulberry Street United Methodist Church in Macon, Georgia, the mother church of Georgia Methodism.

Prior to joining in ministry with Mulberry Street, Ted served Eastman First UMC for five years, bringing the church into partnership with its local community. That work, including serving as chair of the board and president of the local chamber of commerce, led to his recognition as one of Emory University's Forty Under Forty for 2021.

Ted holds a Doctor of Ministry (2021) and Master of Divinity (2015) from Emory University's Candler School of Theology, a Master of Education (2009) from James Madison University, and a Bachelor of Arts (2006) from Berry College. He has also served in ministry positions at Adairsville First UMC in Adairsville, Georgia; Reinhardt University in Waleska, Georgia; Vineville UMC in Macon, Georgia; and the Baldwin County Circuit in Milledgeville, Georgia. Prior to joining the ministry, Ted served in higher education positions at Mercer University, James Madison University and the University of West Georgia.

Ted is married to Dana Mire Goshorn, and together they have two sons: Jackson (twelve) and Carter (seven). They love to travel, hike in the mountains, and play games together. Ted is an avid reader, a runner, and sometimes an old car tinkerer. He loves spending time with friends, family, and finding new ways to have an adventure. To keep up with Ted, visit TedGoshorn.org.

CPSIA information can be obtained
at www.ICGtesting.com
Printed in the USA
JSHW072058271122
33871JS00003B/8